Stefan Henkel

Identification and motivation of high potentials to keep their intellectual property in the company

Anchor Academic
Publishing

Henkel, Stefan: Identification and motivation of high potentials to keep their intellectual property in the company. Hamburg, Anchor Academic Publishing 2013

Buch-ISBN: 978-3-95489-136-8
PDF-eBook-ISBN: 978-3-95489-636-3
Druck/Herstellung: Anchor Academic Publishing, Hamburg, 2013

Bibliografische Information der Deutschen Nationalbibliothek:
Die Deutsche Nationalbibliothek verzeichnet diese Publikation in der Deutschen Nationalbibliografie; detaillierte bibliografische Daten sind im Internet über http://dnb.d-nb.de abrufbar.

Bibliographical Information of the German National Library:
The German National Library lists this publication in the German National Bibliography. Detailed bibliographic data can be found at: http://dnb.d-nb.de

Hermannstal 119k, 22119 Hamburg
http://www.diplomica-verlag.de, Hamburg 2013
Printed in Germany

DEDICATION

Thank you to the most important pillars of my life: my girlfriend, my sister and my parents.

Lea, you are everything for me. Thank you for your love and understanding.

Katrin, you are the best sister I could have. Thank you for all the advice you always give me.

Mom, thank you for everything. You always run errands for me.

Dad, thank you for everything, too. I remember you saying 'always do your best'.

I think I have done it to our satisfaction.

Now we get to the next step…

Further I want to thank Prof. Dr. Andreas von Schubert for coaching me. Thank you for giving me the opportunity to be a small academic participant to the intellectual property management of high potentials.

Thank you, Prof. Dr. Kai Neumann for all the important advice. It has been an honor to learn from you.

ABSTRACT

21 percent of employees have no emotional attachment to the employer, 66 percent will be the call of duty.[1] The figures have almost doubled since 2001. [2]

To counteract this trend, it is important to identify and motivate high potentials to retain them in the company. This primarily concerns the highly dedicated staff, but also the tacit knowledge of the employees that is not explicitly written down.

The author chooses the following title for his Master-Thesis, to take up this subject of economic scientific: Identification and motivation of high potentials to keep their intellectual property in the company.

On this occasion, it is started in the introduction to the subject and the problem is explained, the objectives of the Master-Thesis are presented and it will set a demarcation issue.

Then it is shown how a simple method can identify high potentials.

Chapter 3 describes the proper motivation of A-staff. This chapter includes case study.

The following chapter is about keeping the previously identified employees in the company in order to exploit the existing potential. The top 10 employee retention tools are presented therein. This topic will also be completed by a case study.

A final conclusion collects all the previously mentioned points and ventures a prognosis for the future.

Appropriate literature used to work on this Master-Thesis is present. A corresponding list of references can be found in section IV: Bibliography.

The author chose the above topic, as it is becoming increasingly difficult in the future, to find, identify and motivate good employees, to keep them in one's own company. The demand for high potentials is unimaginably high. In the end, it is in the interest of the company itself, not to lose the high potentials.

---

[1] Harvard Business Manager, Persuading properly, December 22, 2011

[2] Gallup Study, Gallup Engagement Index, 2011

Therefore there is always the same principle: “Companies are only as good as their employees”.[3] So it should be a prioritized ambition for every company, to employ and retain the best of the high potentials.

[3] Technical university Cottbus, Our claim

TABLE OF CONTENTS

I. LIST OF FIGURES

II. LIST OF TABLES

1 INTRODUCTION

Nowadays the shareholder value is more important than the employee. But many studies show it again and again: The critical success factor for very good and successful companies is, to find, identify, develop and keep the high potential employees.[4]

A further fact is that misacts are very expensive for the company. However, companies, which recruit the most talented, the best and the most qualified employees will profit in every way. A very special gain is these people for the costumers. Long-term employees are usually employees, who are able to bind customers in a particularly way. The reason is very easy, but interesting: Companies have an image of humanity that also deemed to employees as to customers.[5]

As the title suggests, the full recruiting of high potentials needs three steps:

- Recruitment of high potentials

  To avoid spending money unnecessarily, it is important to recruit the right staff. Employees, who leave the company after a few days or months are very expensive. There are many several tools in order to find the suitable staff.

- Identification and developing of high potentials

  Chapter 2 describes how to identify the high potentials. There is an easy method to split the employees to different groups, in order to identify the best staff. Actually not many companies use the ABC approach to identify the As, Bs and Cs.

  Further it is important to develop all employees' skills – if possible – especially the high potentials. There are also a lot of tools. The most effective methods are appraisal interviews and management by objectives.

- Keep the high potentials in the company

  It is a special ability to bind especially the A-employees to the own company. It increases the value of a company tremendously, when they have long-term employees. We remember the words, which are also written in the abstract: "Companies are only

[4] H. Janssen, Recruit, develop and keep the best employees, 2011, page 8
[5] T. Tomczak, J. Kernstock, F.-R. Esch, An. Herrmann, Behavioral branding, 2012, page 348

as good as your employees.[6] Currently, unfortunately most of the time only the big companies can manage this topic. Mostly they have an own development department, especially for this mission. In the future there will be almost no company without development department.[7]

1.1 INTRODUCTION TO THE TOPIC AND PROBLEM STATEMENT

It creates not only bad mood and stressed working atmosphere, if an employee adopts. It is also expensive for the company. The main reason for a mental notice is a deficient human resources management.[8]

The increasing time and performance pressure,[9] which is deplored by many employees and labor advocates, calls for maximum performance of staff and executives. Is it possible to call up this desired performance day by day?

There are 63 percent of staff, who have no real commitment to the company and 23 percent of staff, who are actively uncommitted.[10] If we believe in these facts and figures, every fourth person has noticed internally. Annually the German economy pays about 122 billion Euros for the missing motivation of the employees.[11] Employees without direct commitment to the company are frequently ill and spread their displeasure. Only 14 percent of the staff has a high commitment to their company. Therefore it is most important to identify and select this 15 percent. These are the employees who are responsible for the success of the company.

Accordingly there are three problems to be solved by the company:

- Find, indentify, develop and keep the 15 percent staff
- Try to improve the performance of the 63 percent staff
- Detach from the 23 percent staff

---

6 Technical university Cottbus, Our claim

7 PricewaterhouseCoopers, The future of work in 2020, May 2010

8 I. Young, Mental models, 2011

9 O. Svenson, A.-J. Maule, Time pressure and stress in human judgment and decision making, 1993, page 317

10 Handelsblatt, Lack of motivation costs companies billions, March 06, 2013

The following chapters show how to do this. Also there are two case studies to understand step by step how it works to identify, motivate and keep the intellectual property of high potentials in the own company.

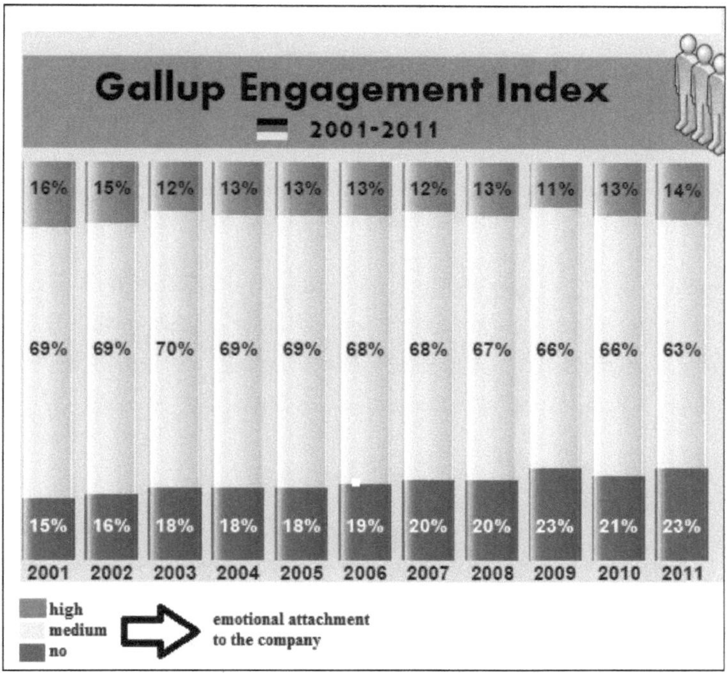

Figure 1: Gallup Engagement Index
Source: Own representation, in dependence on: Gallup, One in four employees has noticed internally, 2011

1.2 OBJECTIVES OF THE MASTER THESIS

The main objective of the Master-Thesis is to show how important it is to have an integral recruitment. In most companies the process of recruitment is only: Hire an employee and let him / her work. Of course – but there are not absorbed in the topic at all – everybody can imagine that this way of recruiting will end in a termination.

Therefore it is my personal objective to sensitize the employees and employer that there is more to this than just hire and fire. At the beginning it is important to select the right employ-

[11] Gallup study, One in four employees has noticed internally, 2011

ee. Try to get him / her in the 15 percent group, the commitment group. Then it is really important to motivate the employee to keep him / her in the own company.

Imagine: There is an employee who has been working already 20 years in the same company. In order to work 20 years in the same company there must be very good motivation. But if the employee decides to change the job or the company – you will lose him / her. It is expensive for the employer. The company will not only lose a (A-) staff member, the company will also lose the intellectual property of the employee. Hereby the company will lose all the information which is not written down. This is the reason why it is so expensive to lose a (A-) staff member.

So it is an objective of this Master-Thesis to discuss identification and motivation of high potentials and how to keep their intellectual property in the company which is important to any interested managing director or human resources manager. I hope a lot of managers will read it, think about it and operate with the case studies in their own companies.

1.3 TOPIC DEMARCATION

The following Master-Thesis is about identification and motivation of high potentials to keep their intellectual property in the company.

As the title already indicates, the text is divided into three main chapters:

- Identification of high potentials

  It is not the object of this Master-Thesis to work on direct recruitment threats. Starting point is that the company has already recruited their employees. At this point the author starts to show how important it is to know what kind of employees are working in his / her own company. Hereby it will show an easy method to arrange the employees in three groups. This arrangement will prove with some examples relating to behavior, personality traits and social skills. Concluding this chapter the author shows how important are these two special management tools: Appraisal interviews and management by objectives – for the employer as well as for the employee.

  Further topics, like how to find the right recruitment strategy or how to handle a job interview are not topics of this Master-Thesis.

- Motivation of high potentials

Most studies want to show how the employer can motivate the employees. Nowadays everybody knows the things with which one you can motivate the employees – for example: short-term with money, or long-term with opportunity for advancement.

Therefore in this Master-Thesis the author thinks outside the box and shows even some facts which are basis for motivation. It is really important to understand how motivation works and under which preconditions.

In a case study the author gives a guidance how the employer can increase the motivation of high potentials.

It is not a topic of the Master-Thesis to select suitable motivation tools. Neither it is a topic of the Master Thesis to demonstrate the effects of motivation.

- Keep the intellectual property of high potentials in the company

The most important fact in this chapter is to show that it is very essential to keep the intellectual property in the own company. There is a lot of knowledge which is not explicitly written down. When the employee leaves the company, he / she also takes the intellectual property. In most cases it is very expensive for the company. Therefore it should be one of the most important tasks in each company to keep the high potentials in the own company – and also their intellectual property.

In this chapter the author does not write about terminations of employees which are not important for the company. Certainly in each company there are a lot of employees who only come to get their money at the end of the month. Sooner or later the company should break away from this kind of employees, but it is not a topic of this Master-Thesis.

The author declares the top 10 of retention instruments. Also some of these tools are motivational tools. In this chapter the author only uses retention instruments. The author summarizes this chapter with a case study about how to keep intellectual property in one's own company. The case study should be used as guidance for all human resources mangers or managing directors in order to realize how important it is not to lose the A-staff.

The Master-Thesis does not show the effects of losing A-staff. In order to demonstrate how important it is to keep the high potentials in one's own company, the losing A-staff topic will broach. But it is not a separate topic in this Master-Thesis.

2 IDENTIFIACATION OF HIGH POTENTIALS

The introduction already suggests that the correct identification of high potentials is one of the most critical facts for the company's success. According to a study of Gallup Business Consulting there are on average only 14 percent of high potentials in each company. This group is the A-staff. Further there are 63 percent followers. They work to rule. Most of them could also be A-staff member, but there is missing something. So the employer has to try to improve their work performance. Last but not least there are 23 percent of employees who have already terminated emotionally. Each employer has to detach from this C-staff. They harm the company.

Therefore it is critical to success to identify the A-staff, B-staff and C-staff in order to make right decisions as a managing director.

In order to classify the groups the author uses the ABC approach. Further tools in this chapter are the appraisal interview and management by objectives.

2.1 SYSTEMATIC IDENTIFICATION OF HIGH POTENTIALS

High potentials tend to rise up out of the crowd and achieve stellar results relative to their peers. But to identify them formally, managers must generally communicate, utilize multiple methods of assessment and compare the results with known criteria that are associated with a specific leadership level. The results of these assessments provide guidelines for training and mentoring a high potential to take on greater leadership responsibilities and build strengths. In a further chapter the author shows that there is an easier method to define the high potentials of a company, the ABC approach. Certainly the most managers use the old standard tools, but nowadays there are instruments which are faster, easier, cheaper and more effective.

Employees who are part of high potential development programs often find themselves under continuous scrutiny.[12] These aspiring leaders face one of the most challenging stages of their professional life as they try to understand their environment, set goals and prove their worth.

---

[12] R. Rodriguez, Latino talent, effective strategies to recruit, retain and develop Hispanic professionals, 2008, page 151

Therefore there are conflicting opinions over whether it's beneficial to inform employees of their high-potential status. Informing employees is a powerful indication that the company values their contributions to the business and believes in them enough to invest in their future. This opinion is furthered by the suggestion of a greater risk that if not told the employee will resign and move on to an organization that will recognize and develop their talent.

The motivation for confidentiality of high potential status also is compelling. Companies risk creating a three class system: A-staff, B-staff and C-staff. The employer or manager creates divisive resentment throughout the company. Either way, high potential employees even tend to know their potential, whether they are officially told or not. Most organizations today are of the opinion that if the high potential is not told by them, someone else eventually will.[13] This could be the way to lose an A-staff member. Therefore the actual research status says to be open with all employees in every sense.

2.1.1 ABC APPROACH TO EMPLOYEE CLASSIFICATION

For the assessment of customer value in marketing customers are often categorized as A-customer, B-customer and C-customer.[14] The largest revenue and profit will realize with the A-customers. The B-costumers usually form the majority and are regular loyal customers with an average revenue and profit. C-customers are often customers with small or micro transactions, a lower company binding and staff attrition rate.

a. Tenability of ABC approach

Basically, the ABC approach raises the question if the method is ethically permitted.[15] Can and is it allowed to classify employees like customers – maybe this is the question on which critics can get a word in edgewise.

But why not – with such a tool companies pay not the patter merchant but the high potential. It is a fact that high potentials are the people, who are responsible for the success of the company. Employees, who are identified as C-staff are counted as losers, because they damage the company.

---

[13] R.-M. Fulmer, J.-L. Bleak, The leadership advantage, 2008, page 90
[14] D. Paff, Understanding, wining and inspiring costumers, 2006, page 44
[15] J. Knoblauch, J. Kurz, To find and keep the best employees, 2009, page 44

The ABC approach should not be used as a tool for rating the human himself, but it should be used as a tool for rating the performance of each employee. This is indeed a big difference.

A further critical point is that the team building is just a task of the manager. The manager decides by himself which employee should be in which group. There could be some facts why an employee is certainly a B-staff member or C-staff member. For example, the employee has not yet the right qualification to do the job or the performance is not yet good enough to be an A-staff member. There could be also a lot of soft facts, like being worried about the job, psychotic topics or personal difficulties. Of course, there are many more facts why employees are not yet in the A-staff category. In this case, the crucial fact is that a good and socially competent manager will search for the reason why exactly this employee is a B-staff member or C-staff member. The managers have to seek the dialogue to the employee, help to eliminate problems and try to increase the performance of the employee's work, provided the employee is willing to do this.

b. Difference between cannot and do not

According to the last sentence in the previous section, it is really important for the manager to find out if the employee is unwilling to rise up to a higher group or if the employee has not the ability to rise up to a higher group. The latter can be changed. Employees who are not able to deliver the expected performance should get some help or easier tasks. Employees who are unwilling to work are often conscientious objectors. In this case the manager should break away from the relevant employee.

At this point it should be mentioned again, that the ABC approach is not a list of naming and shaming. It is only a management tool to identify the A-staff, B-staff and C-staff. Therefore it is not appropriate to post a list with the groups and names on the bulletin board.

c. Criteria of the ABC approach

In an economic study Prof. Dr. Rolf Wunderer found out, that there is following classification:[16]

14 percent co-entrepreneur: They are entrepreneurial qualified and motivated.

31 percent follower: They are entrepreneurially motivated, but not yet qualified enough.

39 percent routine workers: They do their work to rule, earn their money, but they not do more than required.

16 percent internally termination: They damage the company and do not contribute to value creation.

In this Master-Thesis the author refers to an ABC classification. Criteria to get an excellent classification could be hard facts and soft facts.

- Hard facts: Knowledge, individual skills, experience, qualifications, core competences, etc.
- Soft facts: Personality, character, working morale, social skills, personality traits, etc.

These are some facts which can be used to classify the A-staff, B-staff and C-staff.

Certainly there is the rule: 20 – 70 – 10.[17] The top 20 percent of employees are rewarded with bonuses encourage the middle 70 percent, fire the poorest 10 percent. An extreme form of performance evaluation, but the principle is correct.

Leaders must ensure that their team pulls together. And they need to reward performance, as consistently as they have to punish the opposite. Because one lazy person could be enough to demoralize the whole team.[18] One of the latest studies about this statement comes from the psychologist Benjamin Walker, Australian School of Business. He had 158 students in 33 teams to solve various tasks. Result – even it was only

16 Prof. Dr. Rolf Wunderer, Institute St. Gallen, The foursome classification, 1997-1999

17 J. Welch, General Manager of General Electric, 1981-2001

18 Jossey-Bass, Team building, 2007, page 56

one dissenter, who destroyed the discipline of the other members. At first worsened the performance, then the mood. Even if the remaining team members are highly motivated, the loafer had not be compensated. Manager should primarily consider following three characters:[19]

- Freeloaders: They always submerge in group projects.
- Permanent whiners: They always badmouth the group projects.
- Intriguers: They always denouncing other group members.

Even if it is uncomfortable: Leadership means just to punish repeated misconduct.

In this context Jack Welch makes the statement that a C-staff member is too expensive for any company even he / she works free of charge.

Also, the author backs the prejudice that A-staff always are managers, B-staff always are operators and C-staff always are assistants. You can find an A-staff member in each position in the company. A simple example for understanding: A manager, who is convinced by appearance and eloquence in the first impression, can also be only a B-staff member or C-staff member, when he / she does not react to others' ideas and the interests of the company are not as important as the own career or any salary increases. On the other hand there could be a call center member, who always enthuses the costumers with affability and service knowhow. This call center member is able to win angry customers back. He / she is a figurehead for any company. Essentially the call center member – even he / she is not a manager – can be more important for a company than an executive.

Certainly there are many companies with just a few A-staff members. These companies try to get rid of the best employees. Often the managing director thinks that A-staff is most expensive, career oriented and claim too much leadership. Often they say B-staff is more important. B-staff do their work, shut up and are more easy-care. But when you think about the top lines, you will arrive at the decision that average companies want average employees and average employees treat their customer just averagely. This is one of the reasons why it is most important to keep the A-staff in one's company.

[19] B. Walker, Extreme personalities in teams, Annual meeting of the academy of management, 2011

In order to find the high potentials of the company the managing director has to answer the following questions:[20]

- Which employees are valuable for the company?
- Which core competences are required for which position in the company?
- Which requirements are critical to success of the company?
- Who is right for the team and for the managers?
- Which social skills and which expertise are important?

d. A-staff

A-staff members are the top employees of the company. They have above average willingness to perform and a high identification with the company and its products or services. They have an above average commitment, they are action oriented and interested in their advancement. Their motivation is not only monetary, but also satisfaction in the work. It is also these people who are responsible for the working climate and they are always there if you need them.

A-staff members are the most important employees for every company, even in many cases indispensable if the loss of an A-staff member damages the company. Basically every employee is replaceable. But the intellectual property of the high potential is lost. In order to keep them in the company, there must be special plans and targets. The author writes about these facts in chapter four.

High potentials often have a high and pronounced motivation. A distinction is drawn between intrinsic and extrinsic motivation. Intrinsic motivation comes from inside, extrinsic motivation depends on external factors and incentives. This is further explained in chapter three. A-staff employees have a very pronounced intrinsic motivation. They have a special inside drive, because they are enjoying their work.

There is a further classification inside the A-staff group, made by Jim Collins:[21]

---

[20] G.-W. Bohlander, S.-A. Snell, Managing human resources, 2010, pages 13-15

[21] J. Collins, Summary: Good to great, November 01, 2011

- Business leader: Personal modesty, professional assertiveness to sustainable excellence and strong entrepreneurial
- Effective manager: Engagement, successful implementation of a clear and compelling vision, stimulating higher performance standards and action and results oriented
- Competent manager: Organizing people and resources for the effective and efficient implementation of specific targets, successful planning and organizing, encourage employees to performance
- Team member: individual ability, effective team member, strong team player and enthusiasm for new project targets
- Talented employee: productive contributions, good work ethic and takes more satisfaction in execution than in leadership

In order to identify which A-staff member corresponds which group, you can create an assessment form with all the above points. Following that you assess the criteria with high gear, average or little discernible.

e. B-staff

Members of the B-staff provide robust and reliable performance. This kind of work corresponds with the specification and it is expected from them. Even they have social skills, which do not cause problems. You cannot find particular enthusiasm assets, boisterous standing up for new ideas or own training proposals, as with the A-staff members. B-staff build the core of each company. They are usually 60-70 percent of the employees.

Since the B-staff is the middle class of the company you have to distinguish:[22]

[22] J. Collins, Summary: Good to great, November 01, 2011

- B+ advancement potential

  Some examples to identify a B+ member could be: An employee shows eligible talents in a project, an employee shows a rising performance curve, targets are exceeded, positive feedback of customers and suppliers, etc.

  For good and all stamp B-staff as average staff is not the right way. You always can find B-employees with the potential to become an A-staff member. Often there are just private or situational reasons which prevent them. The reasons could be varied. It is the business of the line manager to find out if it is possible for the employee to advance or relegate.

- B- relegation potential

  Managers should give B-employees prospects in order to prove themselves. Regular talks, exact target agreements and inclusion in promotional programs are some tools to advance even the B- employees. Some examples to identify B- employees as willing to rise up are: Active and increasing interest in further education, increasing initiative, submitting proposals, active participation in meetings, etc.

Generally there are also B-staff members who want neither to become an A-staff member nor become a C-staff member. Furthermore they are the group who just work to rule – no more and no less. Often in this group there are also employees who have set their targets in life and priorities in another way.

f. C-staff

This group of employees is also called as Low performer or nine-to-five jobber. Characteristic for this group are low motivation, work is rather annoying rather than a challenge. The only reason to work is to get money in order to support their livelihood. Vacation plans or overtime payments are even more important than work.

The proportion of C-staff should not be more than 10 percent in each company, but often it is a lot more.

Generally the manager has to think about the application range of the C-employee. Often they are used incorrectly. The manager has to maintain the dialogue – maybe it is possible to use the employee otherwise. Following tools can be used to a judgment:

talent oriented trainings or conveyor measures, job rotation or job enrichment, inclusion in project groups, new tasks, etc.

ABILITY PROFILES			
	A-staff	**B-staff**	**C-staff**
Vision	Works independently on a vision that is not only good but can be implemented	Thinks visions not through, even visions are not really realistic	Is rather backward than forward thinking
Leadership	Likes the change and is able to initiate and communicate them	Cautions change in small steps	Averse to change
Action	Passionate working, rapid decisions, 55+ working hours per week	Sometimes motivated, averagely committed, about 40-50 working hours per week	Very different working pace, about 35-40 working hours per week
Independence	Overcomes obstacles, sets new standards, introduces a new mission statement	Often finds own solutions	Needs exact instructions
Customer reference	Highly sensitive in order to satisfy customer requirements	Knows that customer is king, but not so action oriented as A-staff	Misjudges needs and demands of customers
Colleagues / employees	Is not afraid of confrontations, is ready to break up with C-staff	Can live with own second class	Are not able to think target orientedly important things

Teamwork	Works focused and result oriented in teams	Does a little for the success of the team	Kills / weakens the motivation of the team, uncontrolled individual actions
Achievement of objectives	Exceeds expectations	Achieves the objec-tives	Seldom achieves the objectives
Integrity	Absolutely clear	Most honest	Seeks its benefits
Communication	Excellent verbal and written skills	Average verbal and written skills	Mediocre skills

Table 1: Ability profiles
Source: Own representation, in dependence on: IHK Potsdam, ABC analysis of employees

2.1.2 EXAMPLES OF BEHAVIOR, PERSONALITY TRAITS AND SOCIAL SKILLS OF DIFFERENT EMPLOYEE GROUPS

Specific behaviors often illustrate and characterize the differences of performance better than old profiles or assessment models.[23] Following the author shows some occurring daily behaviors of A-staff, B-staff and C-staff.

a. A-staff

- Welcomes new suggestions and ideas, stands behind it and know how to imple-ment
- Visits disgruntled customers personally – even after work – and try to satisfy the customers and win his confidence with specific measures

[23] H. Kasper, W. Mayrhofer, Personality management, leadership and organization, 2002, pages 255-288

- Prepares for meetings, asks interesting questions and are interested in the impact of the work
- Wants to learn more about objectives and impacts of the operation, are interested in developing and improving the talents and potentials and wants to work practically
- Interprets criticism as a learning opportunity and improves the performance in practice
- Knows that excellence is only possible in a committed team and considers the success as a team effort
- Accepts mistakes and failures, tries to find out the reason for failure and tries to make it better next times, does not call the others to account – rather oneself

b. B-staff

- Says often why new suggestions and ideas are not feasible and always finds reasons against them
- Apologizes for failures to the costumer and talks to costumers well
- Considers meetings as a required course, takes note only a minimum to do the work
- Perceives trainings as strenuous, doubts about positive impacts, the motivation is average but generally could increase
- Perceives criticism as rebuke and unwarranted, can be easily discouraged
- Appreciates a good team climate, provides average contributions, fun comes first – commitment to objectives comes last
- Investigates failures in the team, from managers or the company, submits reasons why something can / does not work

c. C-staff

- Seldom pipes up relating to new suggestions and ideas, always wishes that it is closing time

- Are not particularly interested whether a customer is lost – calls it pitch and fate, Are again Mondays at leisure or weekend plans
- Perceives meetings as annoying, fears about more work and more responsibility, never asks questions
- Perceives learning and trainings as unnecessary, considers learning efforts as compulsory exercises and special efforts
- Accepts criticism passively, quickly feels personally offended, feels like victims – guilty are the others always
- Behaves negatively in teams and is at distance, Esteems A-staff and B-staff as careerist, who only live for profession and work
- In retrospect they always have predicted failures, likes to take these as an opportunity for passive behavior and poor working morale

2.2 IMPORTANCE OF APPRAISAL INTERVIEWS

The appraisal interview should inform the employee specifically how the manager assesses the employees' professionalism, personality and performance – strengths as well as weaknesses. Even there is also the possibility for the employee to evaluate the manager, the company and the own field of activities.[24]

The appraisal interview is one of the most important tools of leadership and advancement. It is notable for a modern and employee oriented performance management. Even it is an excellent instrument to find out the high potentials as well as keep and motivate the A-staff in the company.

A good interview includes the holistic observation, registration, analysis and appraisal of the performance and potentials of employees in order to achieve the targets.[25]

It is a function of the appraisal interview to go about delicate and personal problems and to deal with the relationship. After the interview the manager should summarize the conversation and seek feedback from the employee, whether the central issues were specifically

---

24 R. Müller, Systematic performance appraisal and management by objectives, 2005, page 126
25 IHK Nordwestfalen, Guide for assessment and appraisal interview, page 3

understood and interpreted. An appraisal interview can also induce management by objectives – read more about this topic in chapter four – or training measures. At any rate there should be a protocol of each interview and a catalog of measures that the interview gets a mandatory character.

a. Function of a appraisal interview

A holistic hold appraisal interview also includes further aspects to achieve an efficient and targeted cooperation. These aspects could be:[26]

- Establishment
- Confirmation and recognition
- Criticism and relationship improvement
- Clarification of ambiguities
- Agreement of targeted advancement (read more about management by objectives in chapter 2.3)

b. Processes and stages of an appraisal interview

PROCESSES AND STAGES OF AN APPRAISAL INTERVIEW	
Introduction	Preparation of a concept with agreed targets, suitable for the human resources management of the company
Catalog of measures	Creation or update of catalog of measures in order to keep current competency requirements and corporate targets
Arrange with managing director	Arrange all measures with the managing director, human resources department and the line manager
Information of employees	Information of employees about processes, targets, contact, innovations, obligations and inclusion of all

[26] R. Müller, Systematic performance appraisal and management by objectives, 2005, pages 126-127

	employees
Invitation to appraisal interview	Invitation to all employees with dates, reasons and function of appraisal interviews
Self-assessment	Distribute a self-assessment to all employees
Appraisal interview	Personal appraisal interviews include preparation, conversation and catalog of measures
Evaluation and analysis	Graphical and numeric representation of performance and behavior of the employees
Creation of catalog of measures	Jointly elaborate and justify the catalog of measures, written record signed by all parties of the meeting
Discussing with line manager	Information about impressions and process of the appraisal interviews
Report to managing director	Conclusion of the appraisal interview including the most important statements and evaluation of performance and behavior
Catalog of improvements	Creation of an improved catalog of measures
Conclusion meeting	Information about catalog of measures to all employees, preparation of the next appraisal interviews

Table 2: Processes and stages of an appraisal interview
Source: Own representation, in dependence on: H. Janssen, Find, develop and keep the best employees, 2012, page 47

c. Various forms of assessment

- Self-assessments[27]

Self-assessments should help the employees to find the ideal work environment, explore their interests, discover themselves, know their opinion and make a good decision.

[27] T. Breisig, performance appraisal, 2003, pages 40-45

The self-assessment is a structured but informal way of getting to know what you really want, what options are available and how to make the best decision for your career.

- Appraisal interview

Talks between employee and manager happen on an almost daily basis. The appraisal interview however offers the opportunity to systematically discuss especially the following content:

i. Discuss work and performance – tasks, work conditions and cooperation

ii. Resolve problems and misunderstandings

iii. Mutually voice acknowledgement and criticism in a factual matter

iv. Agree on measures to boost development and further education

v. Mutually agree on long term targets and focus points

- Big five personality traits[28]

Just like all the other personality tests, the big five was established in order to help in identifying just who you are psychologically in the belief that you cannot change who you are and better still, you can only deliver best if you choose a career that augurs well with your personality traits. As the experts scrutinize the big five personality test, they agree that it is not only universal but that it is also biological.

Norman Warren, a psychologist, formulated this test back in 1963. It has continued to gain momentum and today, many experts and employers agree that it is the best test that brings out the true personality of a person. The five dimensions that this test tends to place an individual's personality are:

---

[28] N. Warren, The big five personality test

TRAIT	DESCRIBTION
Openness	Curious, original, intellectual, creative and open to new ideas
Conscientiousness	Organized, systematic, punctual, achievement oriented and dependable
Extraversion	Outgoing, talkative, sociable and enjoys being in social situations
Agreeableness	Affable, tolerant, sensitive, trusting, kind and warm
Neuroticism	Anxious, irritable, temperamental and moody

Table 3: Big five personality traits
Source: Own representation, in dependence on: N. Warren, The big five personality test

- 360 degrees feedback

"Horses have always understood a great deal more than they let on."[29]

This kind of assessment is very interesting, because it includes both objective assessments and subjective perceptions of the entire work environment. In this method manager, colleagues, employees and customers give feedback about the behavior and the individual performance of the employees who are to be assessed.

Following main objectives pursued by the 360 degree feedback method:

i. Determining the current performance status of various organizational units, such as divisions, departments, teams, etc.

ii. Derivation and implementing strategic measures to develop the performance of specific units

iii. Identification of high potentials of the company

[29] D. Adams, Dirk Gently's holistic detective agency, 1994, page 2

iv. Derivation and implementation of demand driven and sustainable programs for managers and employees

v. Development and implementation of targeted incentives and reward systems

Figure 2: 360 degree feedback
Source: S.-J. Clegg, 360 degree feedback, 2009

2.3 MANAGEMENT BY OBJECTIVES

Management by Objectives is a concept expressed by Peter Drucker more than 50 years ago.[30] This strategy for managing people, which focuses on managing teams based on their ability to complete individual and team targets, has been used in larger organizations since its inception. Small to midsize organizations, however, can also benefit from adopting this strategy, particularly if you also take on the S.M.A.R.T. (specific, measurable, attractive, realistic, and time linked) method of implementation.

There are various objectives which can be pursued:

---

[30] P.-F. Drucker, Management, 1974, page 336

- Targets of standards and performances

  The products, the services and the processes are unchanged for standard and performance targets. A standard target will be defined in order to increase the performance of employees and the result of work. This type of assessment is very important, even interesting, for the company. There should be a high rate of achievement of objectives and consistent results, standards. But to define standard targets is only possible if the performance is measurable. Therefore it is often used for dispositive activities.

- Targets of development

  Targets of development which are most important for A-staff have highest priority, because these targets are motivating and performance enhancing. Reason for developing targets is to bring the employees to a level which guarantees that the demanded performance can be provided. The effect should be to keep and improve the economy of the company.

- Targets of methods

  If the performance results cannot be clearly defined and the focus is more on labor input, there are often method targets. Sometimes these targets are assigned to the behavioral objectives – because targets of behavior even try to get a better result by changing the operation.

- Targets of behavior

  These targets result a strengthening or change in behavior in order to act cooperatively and effectively towards costumers, colleagues or employees and managers – even in order to work more structured and more efficiently. Often behavioral objectives are confined in work objectives. These targets have been classified as development objectives.

- Targets of leadership

  Management targets often affect the leadership and are classified in such cases as behavioral objectives. This also includes the initiation and control of projects, strategic realignment of business units and general management of change management processes.

- Targets of cooperation

  Working in a team with a good climate is a prerequisite of efficiency employment, pleasure and motivation. If the team is perturbed defined objectives can be the first step to improvement.

For any conversation it is important to know that A-staff, B-staff and C-staff generally have different attitudes compared with management by objectives.

- A-staff

  A-staff members are not afraid of performance measurements and liabilities. But that is exactly the opposite. For them targets are a welcome and desired challenge and an opportunity to show their ambitions, talents and abilities. High potentials have an athletic attitude. They want to top the targets.

- B-staff

  B-staff members are generally sceptical about management by objectives. They lack courage and ambition to compare themselves with targets. Often their performance is accidental. Targets are not a motivation, but a control of the manager and a chore.

- C-staff

  C-staff are always not interested in management by objectives. They refuse to participate because they know that the targets will not be reached.

Management by objectives is an excellent tool to keep high potentials in the company and to motivate them. Most employees – even B-staff members – have a desire to know whether they meet the expectations and whether the manager is satisfied with their performance. Management by objectives replies theses questions in an exact and cooperative way. The most important thing is that the targets are not commanded, but the targets are agreed. This proves that there is a corporate culture which counts on cooperation, respect and consensus.

EXPIRATION OF MANAGEMENT BY OBJECTIVES	
General review	• Assessment of the employment situation and the working environment • Assessment of the organization and department
Performance assessment, based on job requirements	• Timeliness of the formulated requirements • Assessment of the performance, based on job requirements
Performance assessment, based on objectives of previous year	• Assessment of achievement of objectives • Reasons for not reaching the objectives
Definition and agreement of working targets	• Definition of required advancements, tilts and potentials in order to assess the targets • Content and timing measurability of the targets • Consent of all parties to the objectives
Definition and agreement of developing targets	• Assistant agreements • Consent of all parties to the objectives
Additional suggestions, concerns and agreements	• Other requests about the cooperation • Assessment of further suggestions, concerns and agreements

Table 4: Process of management by objectives
Source: Own representation, in dependence on: Dr. W. Schröder, Personnel systems, November 02, 2011

Before closing this chapter it must be mentioned that A-staff are always looking only for A-companies. More attractive and efficient a company is, so much more is the chance to get the best employees.[31]

The best companies maintain values which are very attractive for high potentials. Companies find themselves in the role of candidates. High potentials decide for the company which is most attractive, most credible and most interesting with respect to prospects and challenges.

---

[31] PricewaterhouseCoopers, Strategies in the war of talents, April, 2011

3 MOTIVATION OF HIGH POTENTIALS

High potentials are important to the company. Their motivation is essential. High potentials are leaders and are worthy of investment. They are highly motivated, they are looking for advancement and they are impatient and they are looking for rapid development.

Due to the fact that the theories of motivation are generally distributed and partially implemented in the companies, the author describes in this chapter how motivation works, the importance of employment branding and reasons which can cause demotivation. The chapter concludes with a case study about motivation of high potentials.

3.1 HOW MOTIVATION WORKS

Everybody knows the writings of Maslow, Herzberg, McClelland, etc. As already indicated in this Master-Thesis there is a distinction between intrinsic and extrinsic motivation.

Intrinsic and extrinsic types of motivation have been widely studied, and the distinction between them has shed important light on both developmental and educational practices. Intrinsic motivation remains an important shape reflecting the natural human propensity to learn and assimilate. However, extrinsic motivation is argued to vary considerably in its relative autonomy and thus can either reflect external control or true self-regulation. The relations of both classes of motives to basic human needs for autonomy, competence and relatedness are discussed.[32]

Maslow's famous pyramid of needs shows five levels of needs: Physiological, safety / security, social belonging, ego esteem and self actualization. Maslow would probably suggest increasing the social belonging of high potentials by encouraging them to buy into the company with their hearts. Collect them together in one room and have them discuss major issues, or let them meet in outings and in communities. Their egos are so high that they will tend naturally to self Actualization.[33]

---

[32] R.-M. Ryan, E.-L. Deci, Intrinsic and extrinsic motivation, 1985, page 1
[33] A.-H. Maslow, Maslow on management, 1998, pages 88-95

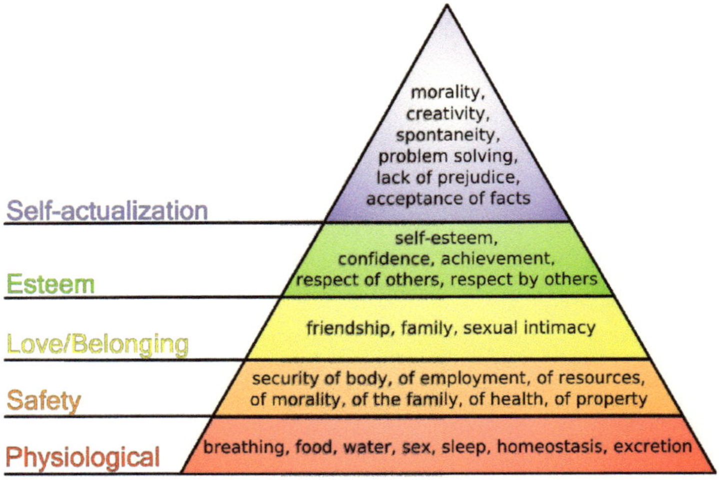

Figure 3: Pyramid of needs
Source: J. Finkelstein, Maslow's hierarchy of needs, October 27, 2006

Herzberg's two factor theory involves hygiene factors like salary, security and fringe benefits and motivational factors like challenging work, recognition and responsibility. Herzberg notes that the lack of hygiene factors can be strongly demotivating. He suggests that we ensure the hygiene factors like salary, security and fringe benefits are safe and secure for the high potentials. That is the irrefutable base. They need challenging work, recognition and responsibility. Give them these and they will be motivated.[34]

[34] F. Herzberg, B. Mausner, B.-B. Snyderman, Motivation to work, 2009, pages 68-74

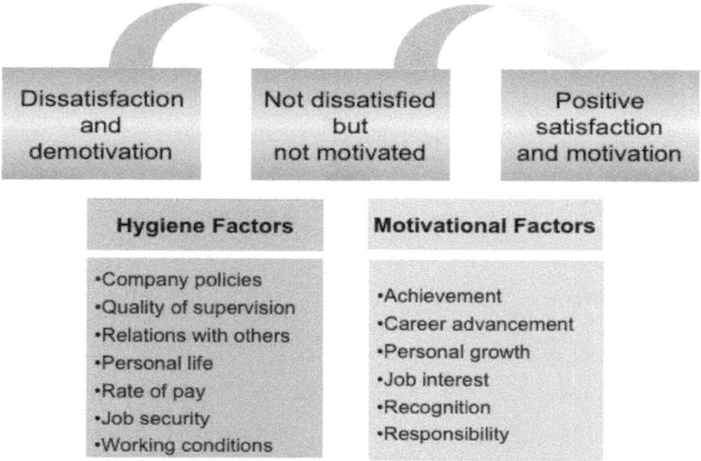

Figure 4: Two factor theory
Source: Penn State, B.-R. Redmond, Herzberg's two factor theory, November 11, 2012

McClelland's theory is also about needs. According to him needs are: Affiliation, power, need to achieve. High Potentials have high expectations of themselves.[35]

To motivate the best employees again and again, it seeks something else: Often A-staff manage to inspire and motivate B-staff and C-staff, especially in team work. In order to get also an acceptable performance of B-staff and C-staff now it is important to motivate even the A-staff more and more.[36]

3.2 EMPLOYER BRAND

The most important brand relationship in your life is unlikely to be your choice of breakfast cereal, mobile phone or car, but the brand you work for, your employer brand. Who you work for represents an extremely important brand choice. This is the brand relationship that takes up most of your time. It's probably the brand with which you're most intensely involved, the brand about which you have most to say (good and bad), and if you're lucky it's a brand with which you'll proudly identify for the rest of your life.

---

[35] D.-C. McClelland, Human motivation, 1987, page 221
[36] Centre for European Economic Research, Specific measures for older employees and late career employment, March 14, 2013

From the organization's perspective, the employer brand sums up the key qualities current and prospective employees identify with you as an employer, whether economic (compensation and benefits), functional (e.g. learning new skills) or psychological (e.g. sense of identity and status). Whether you've defined it or not, you already have an employer brand. The key question is whether you're clear about the distinctive benefits you'd like people to associate with you (commonly described as your Employee Value Proposition), proactive in communicating and delivering against this promise, or happy to live with an unclear and inconsistent employer brand by default.

How people feel about their employer brand is increasingly critical to business success or failure. Leading companies realize its importance in attracting and engaging the people they need to deliver profitable growth. They are also beginning to recognize that creating a positive brand experience for employees requires the same degree of focus, care and coherence that has long characterized effective management of the customer brand experience.[37]

Thoughtful employer brandings answer many key questions of qualified applications that have high demands on their employers:[38]

- Good and positive image of the company
- Identification with the own qualifications and personality
- Modern and relevant for the future branch
- Advancement and development opportunities
- Dynamic, growth oriented, innovative
- Possibility of personal introduction and development
- Positive and respectful idea of man

In Chapter four the author describes what exactly constitutes the attractiveness of the employer.

---

[37] R. Mosley, Employer brand, 2009, page 4
[38] H. Janssen, Recruit, develop and keep the best employees, 2012, page 86

One of the main principles of a good and positive employer branding is that the values are lived. Customers have a very keen nose for the inauthentic, and they will notice just as fast as your employees if there is something phony in the personality you are trying to project if it is not deeply rooted in how the organization feels.

It is one thing to establish the nature of the company's employer brand – what it is and what it needs to be to achieve the business objectives, but it is quite another issue to ensure that it is managed with the same care and coherence as employees would a customer brand. If the employer fail to put in place the management systems and the senior management support for them then the whole employer brand initiative may wither and result in nothing more than some tinkering with recruitment advertising. The marketing concept of the brand "mix" (incorporating all of the controllable elements that contribute towards people's experience of a brand) is just as useful to apply internally as externally. From this perspective, recruitment and internal communication represents only two aspects of the employer brand mix that you may need to address. While the exact constituents of the mix will vary from company to company, the following provides an illustration of some of the most powerful employer brand touch points:

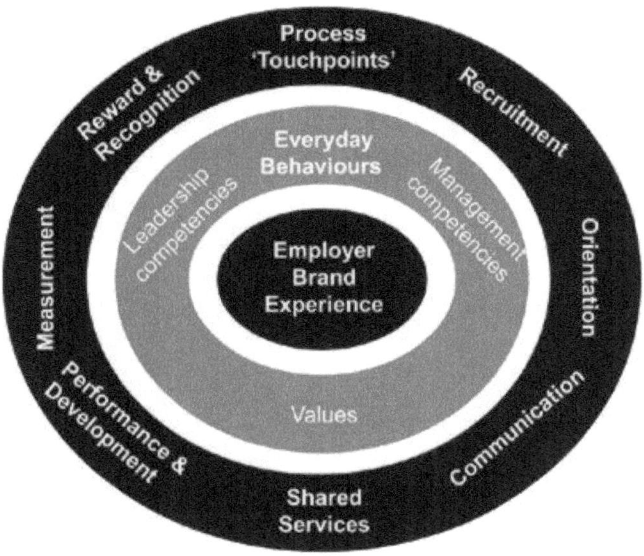

Figure 5: Employer brand experience
Source: R. Mosley, Employer brand, 2009, page 12

It should be added that there is a pleasant effect when a company has a good and positive employer branding. "Since introducing the first global employer brand strategy in 2006, we have not only improved our league table ranking from 45th to 15th in the world's leading 'employers of choice' ranking, but also made a 75 percent reduction in our overall recruitment costs."[39]

3.3 OVERLOAD AND BURNOUT

In this chapter the author writes about overload and burnout. Because burnout often is a disease of the hardworking employees, more and more companies are trying to prevent the loss of motivated employees.[40]

Normally the readers expect in this chapter motivations' tool. According to the author these motivations' tools are known by the managers. Therefore the author consciously decides to write in the following chapters about 'bad habits' in many companies. Especially the A-staff members, the high potentials, try to improve themselves day by day. Continuously to be better or the best can fast and easily end in overload and burnouts.

Hardly would a director, manager or employee publicly admit, that he / she and his / her forces are at the end. Although the numbers have long been pointed out, that this statements could not be true.

---

[39] P. Voser, Chief Financial Officer of Royal Dutch Shell, 2004-2009
[40] L.-J. Gitman, C. McDaniel, The future of business, 2008, page 325

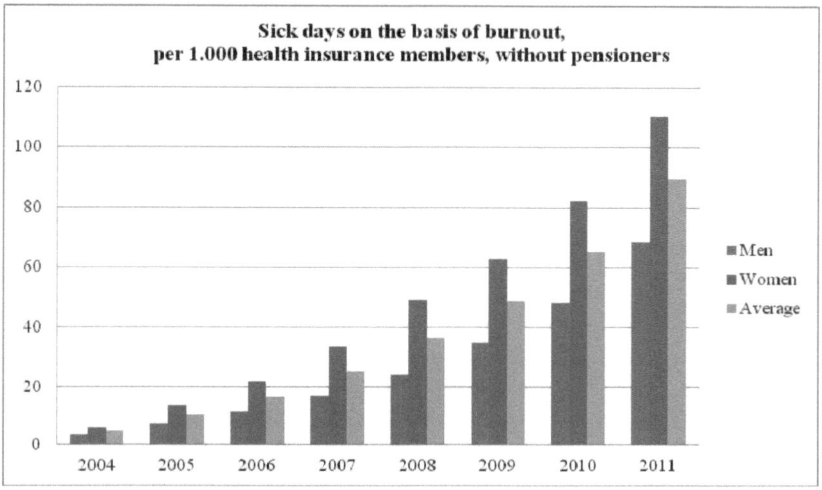

Figure 6: Sick days on the basis of burnout
Source: Own representation, in dependence on: BKK health insurance, 1.800 percent more sick days on the basis of burnouts, 2013

Companies often try to compensate the financial setbacks primarily through cost-saving measures, restructuring projects and job cuts. As a result, it comes to intensification of work for the remaining managers and employees at the same steady increase in complexity within and outside the company. All these factors combined contribute to an unhealthy culture, the employees are confused and it can make them mentally ill in the long term. This problem has worsened again since the last crisis in 2009.

To show the seriousness of the situation in many companies now there is evidence for the first time after an investigation of Asklepios, Europe's leading private hospital chain. Based on the number of its in-patients Asklepios doctors have estimated the amount of people suffering from burnout symptoms to employees of DAX companies in Germany.[41]

Company	Employees in Germany, 2011	Burnout per year, lower limit – upper limit
Adidas	4.500	200-300
Allianz	40.837	2.400-3.400

[41] Konsensus-analysis Asklepios, Annual report, mm-research, 2012

BASF	52.049	1.500-3.400
Bayer	35.800	1.300-2.000
Baiersdorf	5.889	200-400
BMW	73.324	2.200-5.200
Commerzbank	44.474	2.300-3.200
Daimler	167.684	4.900-11.400
Deutsche Bank	24.801	1.400-1.900
Deutsche Börse	1.547	80-100
Deutsche Post	168.108	4.500-11.600
Deutsche Telekom	121.564	3.800-8.900
Eon	35.133	1.800-2.500
Fresenius	45.262	1.200-2.900
Fresenius Medical Care	4.200	100-300
HeidelbergCement	4.500	100-300
Henkel	8.322	300-700
Infineon	7.926	300-600
K+S	10.147	10-20
Linde	7.361	200-500
Lufthansa	67.259	2.100-4.500
MAN	30.187	900-2.100
Merck	10.900	300-700
Metro	91.189	2.800-6.600
Munich Re	24.299	1.200-1.700

RWE	41.632	1.000-2.400
SAP	16.011	700-1.000
Siemens	116.000	3.800-9.000
ThyssenKrupp	68.419	2.500-5.700
Volkswagen	224.851	3.400-6.300

Table 5: Ranking: DAX companies compared – burnout

Source: Own representation, in dependence on: Konsensus-analysis Asklepios, Annual report, mm-research, 2012

In sum, the number of burnout patients is alarmingly high. The aim of the author is to raise awareness. Manager should re-think some motivational tools. Sometimes it is more motivating to get more time to perform instead of giving a higher bonus for extra work. In this connection the obligation of the manager to its employees is very important. There should be a healthy mix between renewed motivation and life balance. It is not always easy, but it is an important responsibility of the supervisors.

3.4 EXECUTIVES AS ENERGY MANAGER

Energy performance in office buildings is part art, part science. Too often, firms place particular emphasis on the "science" – replacing equipment, focusing on new technologies, and relying on sophisticated energy management systems. But the reality is that day-to-day decisions and operations by individuals have as much of an impact on energy performance as the equipment, if not more. Finding ways to motivate, acknowledge, and reward these individuals in a way that aligns their contributions with overall energy goals is critical to a successful effort. This is also an important function of the director or manager.

a. Encourage and discourage at the same time

Every Monday, Tuesday, Wednesday, and Thursday the manager has a tendency to point out how employees can work more efficiently, what else they can do for the company, and how they need to be creating more aggressive revenue goals.

Over the years it is important to learn that criticizing people four days a week does not help them work harder, but at the same time it can push them to quit. So every Friday, the manager should make sure to compliment them on how well they are doing their job and how happy he / she is to work with them. Good managers also do the same thing over the weekend through text messages and emails, which makes them ecstatic and ready to work harder on Monday.

The reason to compliment on Friday is because it is usually a deadline day in which everyone is trying to hit all of their weekly goals. So by saying how well of a job they did, it shows that you appreciate them as well as give them a sense of accomplishment.

b. Dangle a carrot

The best way to motivate employees to work hard while keeping them happy is to dangle a carrot in front of them. For each employee a manager has to figure out what carrot appeals to him or her most.

Whatever carrot you decide to dangle, make sure your employee is emotionally attached to it. Playing off of logic is great, but dangling carrots that play off of emotions are more effective.

c. Give employees a voice

Every employee has feelings and people want to be heard. So when there are meetings or decisions about the company, managers should ask the employees what they think.

Managers don't always have to take their input, but managers are better off asking them what they think as they could come up with a good solution or a point that may never been thought of. Plus this will also help them think outside of the box – so one day employees can just make certain decisions for the manager – so the manager can focus on bigger pictures.

d. Manager's goals should help to accomplish employee's goals

Before any employee starts working, the manager should always ask them their five most important personal goals. These goals cannot be tied to work and have to be purely personal. Once they list them out, the manager let them know which ones the company can help them accomplish.

In most cases the company can typically solve four out of five goals any employee lists out. So as they continue to work for the company over the course of each year, the manager should slowly help them to mark off each of the employees' goals.

The reason to help employees out in their personal life is because it will affect their work life. It does not help to keep both worlds separately, people just have a tendency to mix work life and personal life together.

Surely there are only a few points to help to keep the employees happy while pushing them to their limits. Nowadays many companies know that it is the small things that really make a big difference. The points above show how important it is to know the employees, to bond with them and to find out what makes them happy in life.[42]

3.5 THE LAW OF SERENITY

"God, grant me the serenity to accept the things I cannot change, courage to change the things I can, and wisdom to know the difference."[43]

This prayer is the origin of the law of serenity. On the surface this sounds simple - but it is actually quite time consuming and requires strategic thought and planning. This law can certainly be used for every area of life. The author concentrates only on professional success, as this is an important basis of motivation. There are five effective ways to force the career:

---

[42] N. Patel, How to keep your employees happy while pushing them to their limits, May 18, 2011

[43] R. Niebuhr, Influential American theologian, philosopher and political scientist, 1941

Invest in strengths

Become increasingly aware of the natural strengths that allow to thrive skill sets and capabilities and to make the commitment to invest in them. The ultimate prize is to find happiness in the career and in the work by fueling your strengths and passion.

a. Invest in intelligence and knowhow

Never stop learning. This begins by investing time to acquire the right intelligence and knowhow that will accelerate the career advancement.

Never assume that you do not need to get smarter, wiser and more strategic about how to better manage the career. Get to know the goals of the company and try to find out how you can contribute to achieve them. Build relationships with key thought leaders and get to know what your direct competitors are doing to secure the position you may be targeting.

b. Invest in right relationships

Build a personal advisory board who can properly guide the career goals. Identify the circle of influence.

Invest in how to network the right way. The networking should be viewed as a professional development boot camp. Learn to value the own time and how to connect with the right people. Nurture the relationships that matter most. Give them proper time and attention and foster the most important relationships at all times.

c. Invest in family and personal life

Balance is the key to success – in both business and in life. Contribute to the success of the career by investing in work life balance and dedicating more time and attention to personal and family life.

Invest the right way and manage the career more effectively. Think of the investment as a personal enrichment process: An investment that always works because it focuses on making a better person both in and outside of the workplace.

These are the things which should be focused on. These things can be changed. The author writes not aware of things which cannot be changed – it is up to every person to decide what kind of things can be changed and what not. Therefore this type of motivation is a difficult kind of self motivation which, however, can certainly be supported by experienced and good managers.

3.6 CASE STUDY 'HOW TO INCREASE THE MOTIVATION OF HIGH POTENTIALS'

Subsequently the author describes and solves a case study about the motivation of high potentials. If high potentials change their behavior, special care is required. Either there is a significant problem in the professional environment, within the company – or there is a change in the life situation of the employee which affects the professional. In both cases it is something that performance cannot appear value able or even possible.

a. Initial position

Recently, Susan[44] had a meeting with her supervising manager. Without asking for reasons the manager accused her of a lack of motivation. He analyzed her absenteeism - very often, but always only a few days. It appears to him as Susan would take breaks during the rush hours. The manager closed the short meeting with Susan saying: Everybody has to do his or her work. If it is too much for him / her, he / she has to leave the company.

b. Description of employee

Susan is 42 years old and single parent mother of two kids (5/7). She works as an administrator in the head office for a company which produces garden furniture. She is committed and a responsible employee. Social responsibility is an important value for Susan. Talking about herself she says that she is rarely ill.

If Susan does not feel so good, she motivates herself. However, regularly both kids bring infectious diseases from kindergarten and school. Only one child is ill, then the other and finally Susan. In order to keep the absenteeism as low as possible she tries to stay at home only when it is really necessary.

c. Observations / Susan's decision

Susan was totally surprised about the meeting. Susan did not expect something like that. Her motivation sank instantly. She thought about the medical reports. Susan's doctor always recommended not to work immediately after the sickness. She and her kids should fully recover first.

Susan is very disappointed by the company, especially the manager. At the meeting Susan did not say anything about the manager's statement. Instead, she chooses to put the child and herself in the first place the next time they fall sick. So she will be ill for two weeks, not only for one or two days. At this moment she does not care about who will do her work during her absence.

Following the author describes and solves the case study. This is not the only one and right solution, but it is one way to increase the motivation of high potentials. There are also other ways which can be right and lead to a good result.

d. Requirements analysis

As already mentioned above there can be two reasons for Susan's absenteeism – private reasons or company's internal reasons.

i. Company's internal reasons

Generally performance oriented employees ask the manager for a clarifying conversation. If there is no conversation it is an indication that the current situation is a breach of trust or a breach of emotional attachment to the company. In this case it depends on the good manager to maintain the dialogue between him / her and the employee. It is very important to discuss the situation of the employee, not the situation of the manager or the company. Often it is only a misunderstanding. But generally it is to build or rebuild a new trust. In this case it is the responsibility of the manager to find a solution.

ii. Private reasons

If there are no company's internal reasons for the demotivation, there can only be private reasons. For many managers it is difficult to talk with the employees about private problems and the reasons for demotivation. Often it is difficult enough for the managers to communicate business topics. Therefore managers often say that they cannot discuss private problems. This would not be up to

---

44 The name is fictitious and is irrelevant in the case study

them. But it is an absolutely wrong way of thinking. If there is an employee who needs help, even in the private life – and the employee is also important for the company – the manager should talk with him / her in order to help. Also it is important to know that the manager is not responsible for the solution of the private problems. But often it is possible to help with operational measures.

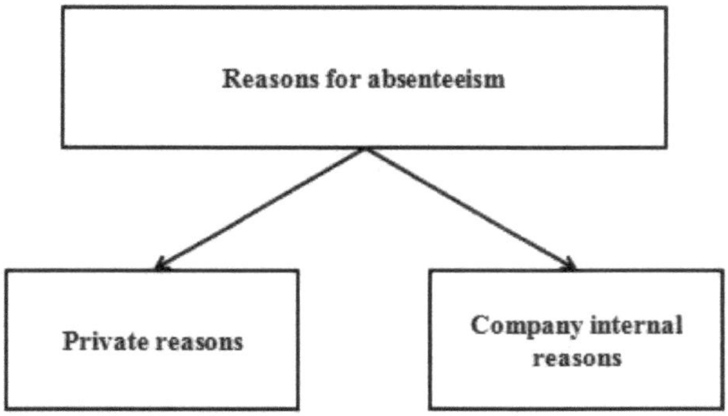

Figure 7: Reasons for absenteeism of employees
Source: Own representation

In this case study the reasons for Susan's absenteeism are only private reasons. Therefore it is important to develop a special action plan to motivate Susan and keep her in the company.

e. Development and action plan

In order to create a development and action plan there are two important measures which should be used in any case: The appraisal interview and management by objectives. The appraisal interview is important to identify the reason for demotivation and bad performances. As already mentioned above it depends on the reason if the manager or employee should look for a dialogue. The meeting should be in a quiet office. The manager should take time for this meeting. Both parties should be open to each other. In this discussion should be reflected the reasons for the lack of motivation and performance.

The next step is management by objectives. Perhaps the current goals have to be re-considered. Alternatively it may be necessary to set new goals. It also depends on the reasons for demotivation and bad performances.

Figure 8: Development from demotivation to motivation
Source: Own representation

f. Results

The most important result is to know that the meeting between the manager and Susan should not have been taken place in this manner. The manager recognized the demotivation and bad performance of Susan. Because the absenteeism was not a problem for Susan, consequently the manager starts the dialogue. Except for this fact everything was right.

The point was that the manager forgot to analyze the reasons for Susan's absenteeism. Therefore the way the manager talked with Susan was wrong. The analysis could also be a part of the appraisal interview which was the above mentioned meeting. Susan could explain her reasons for absenteeism. Both of them together could search for a solution which is acceptable for the company, the manager and Susan.

As they search for a solution together, everybody is eye to eye with it. Therefore Susan's performance should improve again. Perhaps there are possibilities or opportunities to agree on new personal and company's internal goals through management by objectives.

g. Measurements of result

Sometime after the first appraisal interview there should be another one with Susan and the same manager in order to check the absenteeism again. Now there should be another result – acceptable for Susan and her manager.

h. Conclusion of case study

This case study should be an example for directors and managers to motivate high potentials and to keep them in the company. Primarily the case study should show the two most important tools and its effects for motivation: The appraisal interview and management by objectives.

Also the aim of the case study is to clarify that it is positive for the company to motivate their staff in order to keep the best employees in the company.

Generally there are a lot of advantages when employees are motivated. This case study shows that by missing appraisal interviews and management by objectives employees often terminate internally. Appraisal meetings bring positive effects for the employee: Motivation for high performances – and there is also a positive effect for the manager: Accepted as a good manager with very pronounced social skills.

The easiest way for the company to be a successful company is to have a high rate of motivated employees – the easiest way for an employee to be motivated is to be open minded in appraisal interviews and management by objectives – *so how is it possible to run companies without these motivation tools?*[45]

[45] S. Henkel, A question which has to be discussed, emerged in the Master-Thesis "Identification and motivation of high potentials to keep their intellectual property in the company", 2013

4 KEEP THE INTELLECTUAL PROPERTY OF HIGH POTENTIALS IN THE COMPANY

The conventional way to protect intellectual property is to patent it. This gives a company legal protection for the innovative idea. If others want to use it, they must pay a royalty for it. The snag is that the company must publish the idea. This makes it easy for someone in a less lawful country to steal it.

As a result a lot of companies are keeping their most valuable ideas under wraps. But it is not enough. Hackers are cunning and China for example employs thousands of them to steal foreign secrets.[46]

4.1 EMPLOYEE RETENTION

Bring dogs to work, swimming pool including lifeguards, meals free of charge, opportunities for fitness, childcare and even the possibility to get a haircut – these are only a few measures which search engine operator Google use in trying to simplify the life of employees.[47] However these are extreme examples how employee retention works. Some other companies operate with simplified forms of employee retention and even it is not necessary to have a material convenience form of it. Retention management arouses more and more interest of companies and the human resources departments. But it is not easy to comply with normal leadership tools. Often there are many factors which are not included in an employment. Anyway, most managers think they keep the high potential in the company with money. But high potentials are looking for more than money.

The loyalty of employees to their employers is often and mainly a psychological variable. It is often called commitment. Acquired knowledge and specialist expertise in key and expert positions, sound practical experience with tasks, processes and characteristics of the company, the network of relationships internally and externally and costly trainings and incentives are just a few reasons for the importance of employee retention.

Generally the choice of word retention is not optimal. It means to bind the employee to the company and prevent the high potential from leaving the company. As mentioned above, this also contradicts social trends. There are also some experts who say companies do not need

---

[46] R. Johnson, China has found a brutally simple way to steal corporate secrets, February 19, 2013
[47] Google, Life at Google

employee retention if it succeeds into inspiring the employees with attractive labor content, responsibility, self determination or a positive working atmosphere.[48] The focus is on enthusiasm.

Even here are some parallels to customers: Companies which are able to inspire the customers with quality and service do not need customer retention measures.

Of course there are also people with increased binding readiness. Reasons for it could be loyalty, own nature, work ethic and values of life. Employees' motives are drivers:

- No willingness to change the domicile

  Justifications: Sense of place, sports club, friends, etc.

- Family reasons

  Justifications: Avoid changing school, workplace of spouse, etc.

- General fears and concerns

  Justifications: Changes, uncertain risks, disadvantages, etc.

- Maintaining old habits

  Justifications: Need for consistency, fear of change, etc.

- Loss of existing investments in business

  Justifications: Commitment and career goals for the company, etc.

- Risk of losses

  Justifications: Pension claim, bonus, opportunity for sabbatical, etc.

- Company Justifications: Connectedness to colleagues and team, good working atmosphere, etc.

These factors should already be noted in the recruiting process of employees. It positively affects employee retention and therefore reduces the cost of employee retention measures.

---

[48] P. Odgers, Administrative office management, 2005, page 176

Often, however, managers are the guarantors of employee retention. This has the consequence that leadership skills and social skills of managers are crucially important. A manager, who recognizes, knows values and respects the employees are the best guarantors of successful and lasting employee retention. This kind of managers provides perspectives and promotes the employees' careers and advancements. Following factors are manager depending guarantors:

- Employee development with focus on their career and perspectives
- Opportunities to think and act entrepreneurially
- Integration in decisions and innovation processes
- Systematic agreements as leadership tool
- Interesting, promoting talent tasks and challenges
- Security through a good working atmosphere
- Flexible and selectable working hours
- Attractive and custom offers of work life balance

It is important to realize that even these areas are qualitative retention instruments that particularly appeals to employees who are talented and interested in developing. Therefore there are those employees who are interesting for the company – the high potentials. Especially big and successful companies recognize an employee oriented leadership culture.[49]

For example, about 70 percent of the most successful companies explain to practice a culture which is more focused on family, friendly personnel policies and equal opportunities.[50] Especially flexible working hours have a positive effect on the employee retention. Given below are some more answers from employees to the question why they remain faithful to the company:

- Career opportunities and personal development
- Exciting and interesting tasks and challenges
- Good working atmosphere, fun and nice colleagues

---

[49] H.-J. Bullinger, H.-J. Warnecke, E. Westkämper, New organization forms in companies, 2003, page 370

- Good supervising manager who recognizes and appreciates the performance
- Autonomy, freedom and responsibility
- Flexible working hours, fair salary and bonus

These are the most common reasons for the employee to remain in the company. A study of Beckhäuser Staff & Solutions and nobisCum shows following results:

Reasons of retention	**... is important for the employees**	**... is practiced in the company**	**Difference**
Salary	63,4 %	46,4 %	17,0 %
Framework	64,4 %	43,8 %	20,6 %
Perspectives	90,6 %	63,5 %	27,1 %
Working atmosphere	77,2 %	42,9 %	34,3 %
Leadership	95,6 %	54,4 %	41,2 %

Table 6: Reasons for retention of employees
Source: Own representation, in dependence on: Beckhäuser Staff & Solutions, nobisCum, A study of employee satisfaction, page 24

This study shows that there are still many companies which do not focus on their employees. In order to have an employee retention like the big and successful companies it is very important to give the employees voice and listen to them carefully. Only then there could be a chance to keep the intellectual property, especially of high potentials, in the company. The difference between what employees want and what employers give is big enough to attract the employee to one of the big and successful companies. Like mentioned above this is the biggest mistake that can be made by any company. Mostly the most effective and most efficient way – ask the employee – listen to them – implement the suggestions – it is a continuous improvement process for both the company and the employees.

[50] Institute of German economy Cologne, Hire and fire is out, 2010

4.2 TOP 10 RETENTION INSTRUMENTS[51]

The question how to keep and bind the high potentials is complex and depends on the company's individual strengths and offers. If a company offers, for example, attractive working hours, good career advice and support instruments have to move to the center. Other points like salary system or market leadership should be in this case in the background.

This is similar to the high potentials. Especially the high potentials often have individual and personal requirements and expectations which cannot be satisfied with an easy and generally used retention management system. They need a special program. If one needs career opportunities and advancements, the other might need attractive and challenged tasks and freedom at work.

This fact should be considered by key positions. Such individual retention opportunities often result in management by objectives, advancement meetings, etc. Generally employees with an intrinsic motivation are readier to bind to a company than extrinsically motivated employees who need special incentives. The risk of losing employees is much higher among extrinsic motivated employees because it is not always possible to motivate these high potentials with incentives like bonuses, work life balance, etc.

It is especially difficult for small and medium-sized companies to establish effective frameworks for a sustained retention management system. Often they are neither brand products nor famous companies. Often they have locational disadvantages, no attractive salary models and no budgets for a powerful and systematic staff development.

But certainly even small companies could have convincing advantages to be attractive for high potentials. Faster decision making, faster perceiving of high potentials, holistic in getting to know the company, faster development of high potentials' knowhow are such a few advantages. Further there is often more responsibility, better overall insights, more proximity to customers and a better traceability for decision making. Therefore even small companies should set their goals, with respect to retention management and employer attractiveness, in the center of human resources management.

Subsequent to this section of the Master-Thesis you will find the top 10 retention instruments used by the biggest companies in Germany. However, it is not possible for a company to pick

[51] C. Liebhart, Employee retention management and action errors, 2009, page 45

these top 10 tools and think everything will be better now. The choice of suitable instruments is influenced of many factors:[52]

- Staff structure

  The structure of the workforce has a significant influence on the choice of appropriate and effective tools. It depends on the age, marital status, educational level, gender, family background, average length of stay in the company, etc. Therefore attractive working hours or work life balance measures are probably a good choice in the case of employees with children.

- Employee needs

  Employee needs are also centralized. There are employee surveys which are especially revealing. The analysis of used existing human resources services, fluctuation analysis, exit interviews and feedback from appraisal interviews can be important and helpful.

- Targeting of the company

  Often it makes sense to apply different retention instruments to particular segments or function, levels of education, positions and life cycles. For Example, development opportunities and job contents could be more important for high potentials than working hours or well-being in teams.

- Strengths and resources

  It is necessary to clarify which instruments of the company are well equipped and have strengths. For example it could be caring responsibilities (social areas), organizational strengths (work life balance measures), premises (fitness), efficient IT-structure (management of working time models), etc. Even the cost issue is important because some instruments generate high costs, especially in the period of implementation.

52 H.-J. Drumm, Human resources, 2008, pages 381-389

4.2.1 OPPORTUNITIES FOR ADVANCEMENT AND DEVELOPMENT

The first tool is to offer opportunities for advancement and development. This is an important perspective which constitutes a permanent and motivated challenge for high potentials. Therefore it should be thematized and agreed continuously and systematically in order to keep the high potentials in the company. Companies which operate with consistent employee advancement and attractive development programs benefit in several ways. These companies are able to bind talents and capable employees to the company by promoting important core competences, embossing a positive employer branding and increasing productivity of employees. Often it is very interesting for the employees because they would do everything to develop their own qualifications and performance in order to achieve career objectives. Employees who regard opportunities for advancement and development as strong incentives are often high potentials who have good qualifications and high performance.

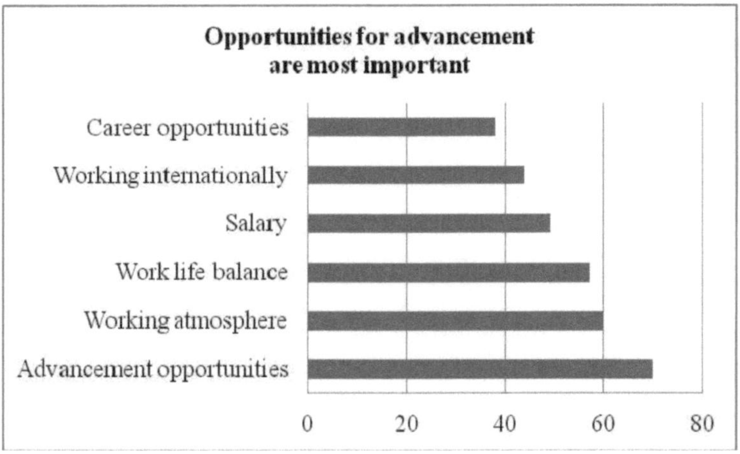

Figure 9: Opportunities for advancement are most important
Source: Own representation, in dependence on: Financial Times Deutschland, Salary is not so important for entrants, Survey of 279 colleges of various disciplines, multiple answers possible, May 20, 2011

4.2.2 PROFESSIONAL TRAININGS

Successful companies offer active and systematic professional training. On the one hand they motivate and keep the A-staff / high potentials, on the other hand they increase the quality and performance of their employees. It is important to create a balance between employees' needs (talent, interests, careers, etc.) and companies' objectives (priorities, core competences, important requirements, etc.). Generally it is a better strategy to promote the strengths and talents of the employees than eliminating deficits and weaknesses. Even it is important to promote the intrinsic, responsible and self-directed learning of A-staff members.

Often it is difficult for the human resources department to manage this successfully. The company wants the best employees – so the employees get professional training. However, this qualifies the employees further. They will be interested in other companies – also there is a high risk of losing high potentials. Should the company decide to promote high potentials further on it is very important to have a well functioning retention management system.

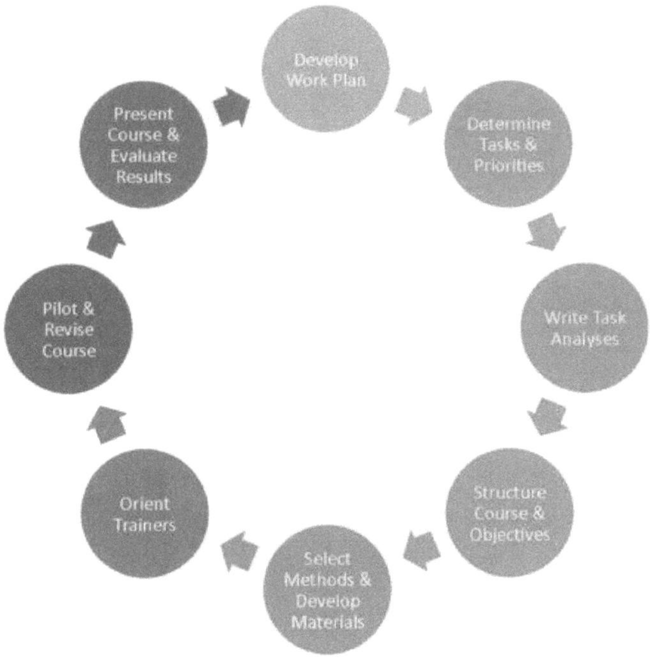

Figure 10: Cycle of professional training
Source: T. Johnson & Associates, September 11, 2011

4.2.3 RESPONSIBILITY SCOPES

High potentials are often responsible employees who do not need instructions. But they want freedom to experiment, make responsible decisions and set priorities. High potentials like and love to assume responsibility. In this way they can influence results which stand for sense of achievement. To realize one's own ideas this is the most important thing for high potentials – and it is also always an incentive to top performance.

There are always two theories which can be applied by managers. Theory X always creates C-staff members. But theory Y improves the responsibility scopes and produces more and more A-staff members. Unfortunately on the contrary there are so many managers who think theory X is the right.

As already mentioned above it is another advantage for the company and the directors and managers. If employees assume responsibility the manager can concentrate on bigger business issues and orders.

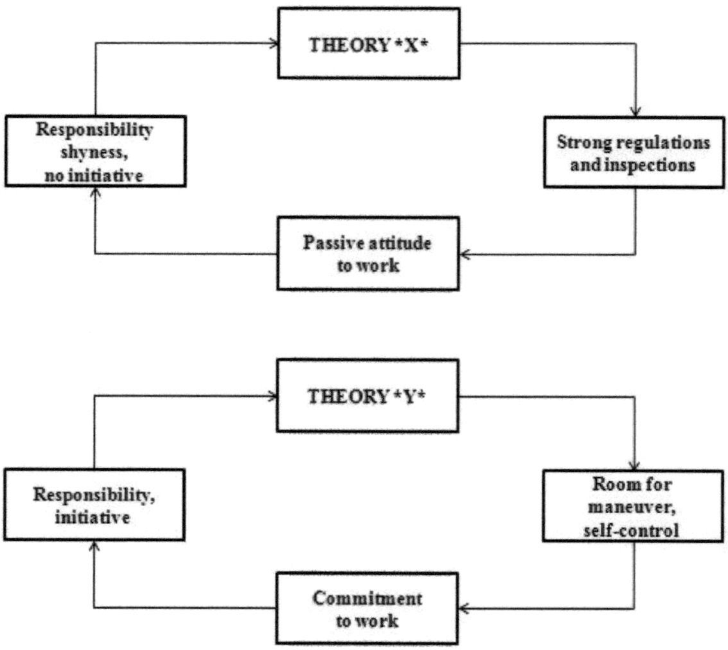

Figure 11: Cycle X and cycle Y

Source: E. Kirchler, Industrial and organizational psychology, 2008, page 111

4.2.4 RECOGNITION AND APPRECIATION OF JOB PERFORMANCE

Praise and recognition push the employees to high performances.[53] This is the same for all employees: A-staff, B-staff and C-staff. High potentials realize that their services are not only recognized but also appreciated. B-staffs are encouraged to produce supererogation and motivation to become an A-staff member. Even C-staff can have pleasure at work and performance. Capable leaders regularly praise. Employee oriented companies often celebrate successes and provide instruments of recognition and gratitude for the special commitment.

Following chart shows that there is always much potential to increase the recognition and appreciation in all businesses.

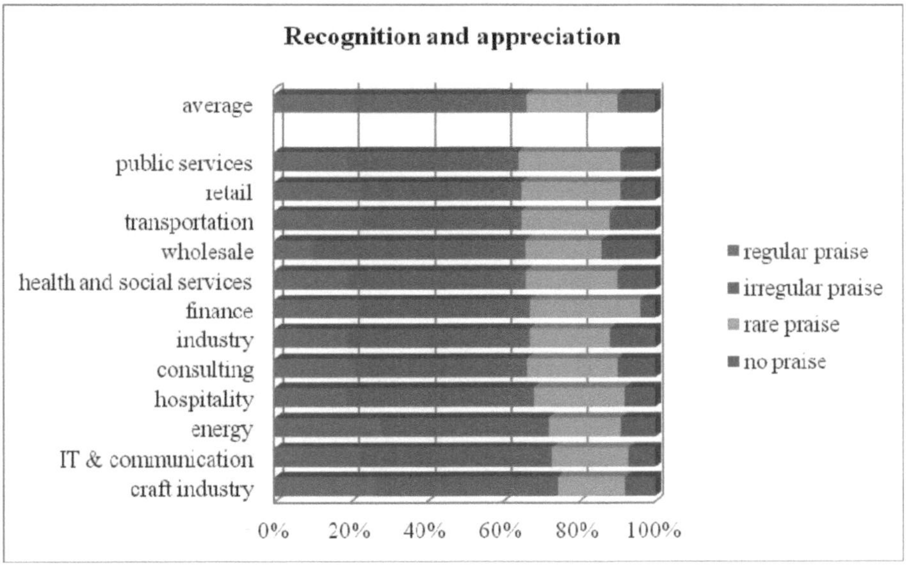

Figure 12: Recognition and appreciation
Source: Own representation, in dependence on: Service value, Recognition and appreciation, September 18, 2012

4.2.5 OPPORTUNITIES TO CO-DECIDE AND PARTICIPATION

Opportunities to co-decide and participation are important and motivated for encouraged employees.[54] Active and ambitious employees, especially high potentials, gladly decide to set

[53] R.-G. Schroeder, B.-B. Flynn, High performance manufacturing, 2001, page 159
[54] Keller Consulting, Motivation, March 01, 2013

their own course. For them it is also important to make their own decisions in as many areas as possible and to be involved in all decision makings. High potentials appreciate when they are asked for their opinion and criticism or to judge opportunities and threats.

4.2.6 PERFORMANCE ORIENTED PAYMENT

High potentials are often motivated by bonuses or extras. The salary is often not on the top of their priority list. But there are exceptions. For this purpose it is possible to introduce a performance oriented and variable salary system which reflects a measurable, concrete and economic esteem. Even it is possible to introduce profit, sales, capital participation or employee stock options. These opportunities increase feelings of responsibility and identification with the company.

For example it is more effective to appreciate the performance of employees by telling personally than by writing an email. Even it is the same for the pay rise. The employee feels a lot better if the manager tells and shows him / her the reasons for the pay rise. A pay rise without pronounced reasons is effective only for a few days. But a short dialogue between the manager and the employee is effective till the next pay rise.

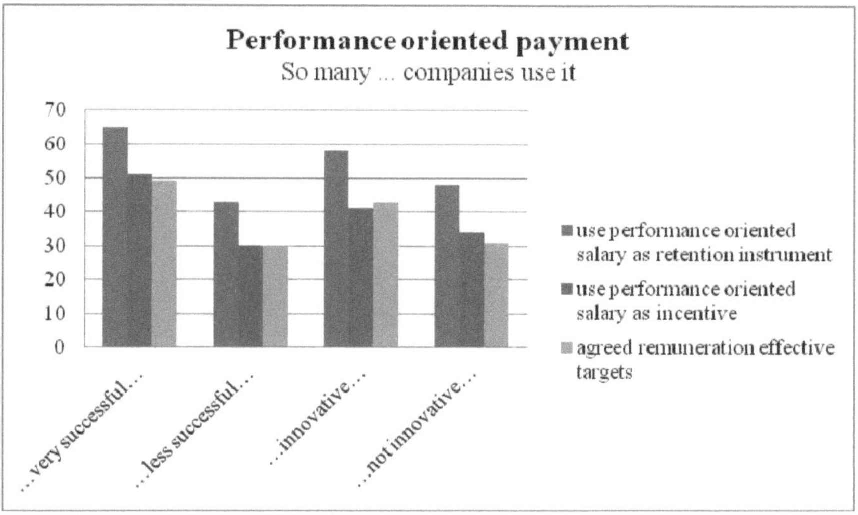

Figure 13: Performance oriented payment
Source: Own representation, in dependence on: Institute of German economy Cologne, Extras for good performance, August 2010
Survey of 1.853 human resources managers

4.2.7 WORK LIFE BALANCE[55]

a. Background of work life balance

Finding a suitable balance between work and daily life is a challenge that all workers face. In particular, families are mostly affected. Some couples would like to have (more) children, but do not see how they could afford to stop working. Other parents are happy with the number of children in their family, but would like to work more. This is a challenge to governments because if parents cannot achieve their desired work life balance, not only is their welfare lowered but so is development in the country. If parents have to choose between earning money and looking after their children, the result is that there will be too few babies and too little employment.

People spend one-tenth to one-fifth of their time on unpaid work. The distribution of tasks within the family is still influenced by gender roles: men are more likely to

---

[55] OECD, Work life balance

spend more hours in paid work, while women spend longer hours in unpaid domestic work. While on average men in OECD countries spend 131 minutes per day doing unpaid work, women spend 279 minutes per day cooking, cleaning or caring. This average difference, approximately 2.5 hours per day, conceals many disparities among countries. For instance Turkish and Mexican women spend between 4.3 and 5 hours more than men working on domestic chores, while the difference is only a little over one hour in the Nordic countries.

b. Employees working long hours

An important aspect of work-life balance is the amount of time a person spends at work. Evidence suggests that long work hours may impair personal health, jeopardize safety and increase stress. The share of employees working more than 50 hours per week is not very large in OECD countries. Turkey is by far the country with the highest proportion of people working very long hours, with more than 40%, followed by Mexico with nearly 30% and Israel with a fifth of employees. Overall, men spend more hours in paid work and the percentage of male employees working very long hours across OECD countries is 12%, compared with less than 5% for women.

c. Time devoted to leisure and personal care

The more people work, the less time they have to spend on other activities, such as personal care or leisure. The amount and quality of leisure time is important for people's overall well-being, and can bring additional physical and mental health benefits. The average person in the OECD works 1 749 hours a year and devotes 62% of the day, or 14.8 hours, to personal care (eating, sleeping, etc.) and leisure (socializing with friends and family, hobbies, games, computer and television use, etc.). Fewer hours in paid work for women do not necessarily result in greater leisure time, as time devoted to leisure is roughly the same for men and women across the 20 OECD countries studied.

As the following chart shows Germany already has a very high work life balance compared to other countries which have more potential to develop. Additionally, in many companies there is also a lot of potential to improve the work life balance.

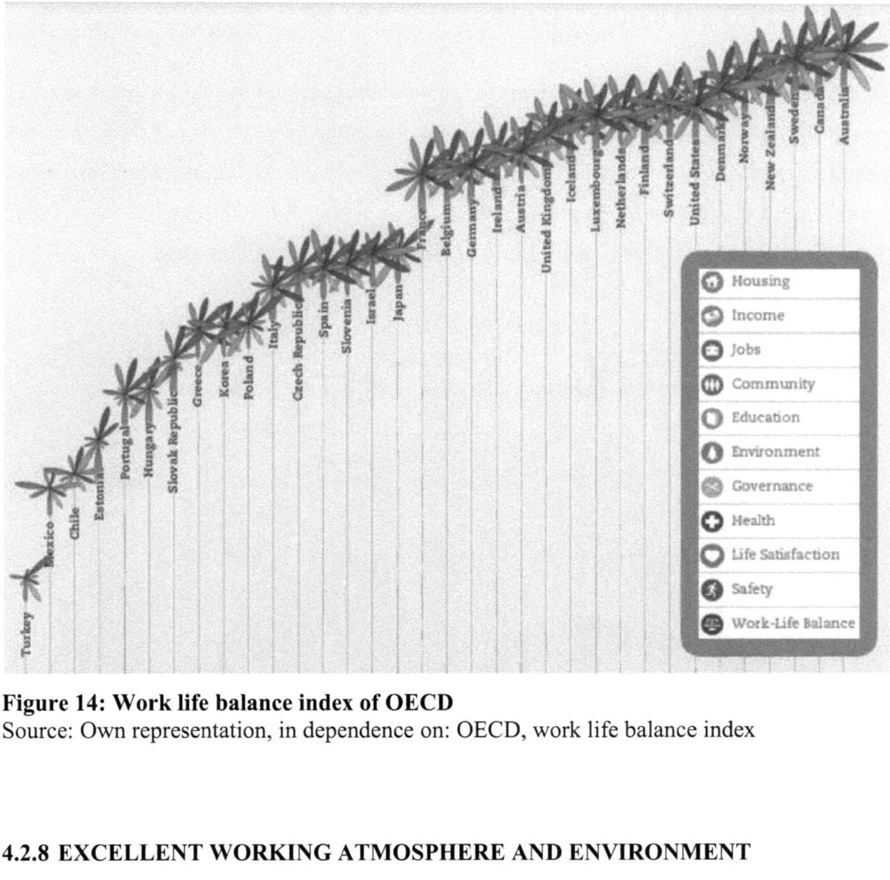

Figure 14: Work life balance index of OECD
Source: Own representation, in dependence on: OECD, work life balance index

4.2.8 EXCELLENT WORKING ATMOSPHERE AND ENVIRONMENT

The working atmosphere and environment is interesting for high potentials if it is varied and inspiring. There should be challenges, opportunities and chances to discover and explore. Visionary companies with a mission know these facts and try to communicate and show them in concepts, behavior and social competence of their directors and managers. A good working environment needs a good collaboration between teams and people and an atmosphere supporting a learning culture. It is even important for managers to know that a team inspired by itself if there is a balanced mix between different cultures and different ages. This promotes the individual strengths of the employees.

Often it is not clever to mix high performance teams with B-staff and C-staff. These employees slow down the whole team, as already mentioned above.

4.2.9 INTERNAL COMMUNICATION

High potentials want to be well informed and be up to date because it is the only way to shape oneself up and take responsibility. Good informative companies prove and show that they take their employees seriously and get them involved in business actions. The chart below shows some examples and opportunities how it is possible for companies to inform their employees. This chart includes many forms of current internal communication.

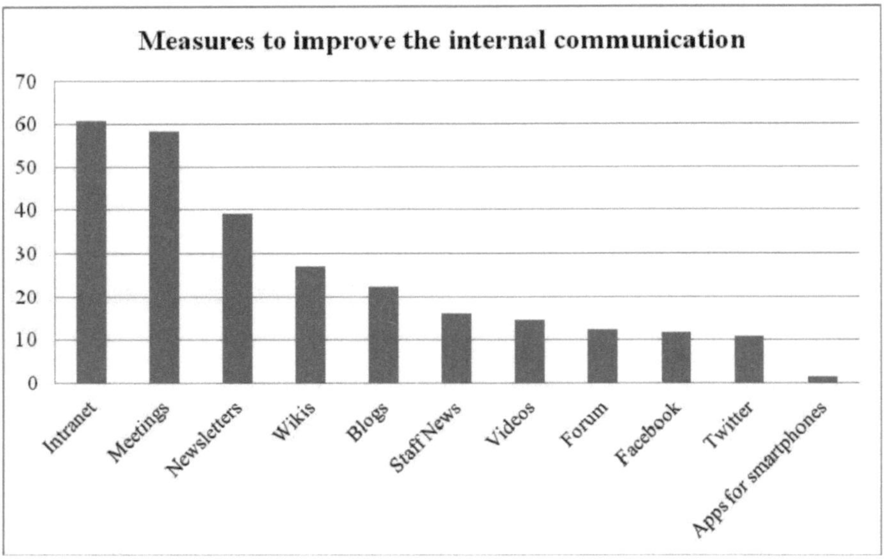

Figure 15: Measures to improve the internal communication

Source: Own representation, in dependence on: Xinnovations e.V., Manager to staff, January 10, 2012

As the chart shows there is much potential for the companies to improve the new technology of internal communications. Nowadays everybody has a smartphone. Therefore the companies should use this way of internal communication. There are some companies which use one of the easiest ways for internal communication, for example BBVA. The BBVA group is one of the world's largest financial institutions. BBVA relies on smartphones to accelerate key processes to improve internal communication and to provide the best possible service to its millions of customers around the world.[56]But also the other methods of internal communications should be used by the companies in order the reach every single employee.

4.2.10 HONESTY AND CREDIBILITY OF THE COMPANY

High potentials prefer trustworthy companies[57] - such companies which stand by their promises and practice and live up to their expressed or implied promise. These companies have the courage to admit mistakes. They openly and honestly communicate the mistakes to their employees, keep career promise or opportunities for new positions and stand by their word. Even these values are important with regard to B-staff and C-staff in order to motivate them. Living up to these values an example is set by directors, managers and the corporate culture.

Therefore it is important to begin with honesty and credibility at the top of the management. If there are lies and deception involved, nobody wants to know how it looks like at the executive level. The employees can only be honest and credible if they can expect the same from their supervisors.

However, only honestly and credibility does not lead to sustainable success of a company.[58]

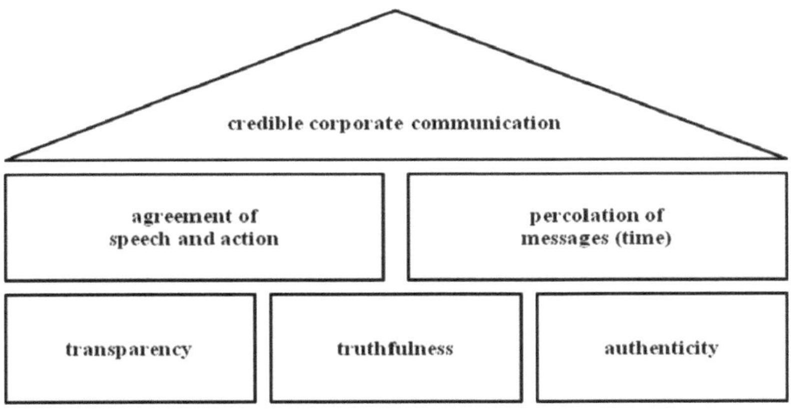

Figure 16: How to create a credible corporate communication
Source: Own representation, in dependence on: Dipl.-Ing. J. Petermann, Weblog easy and personal, February 17, 2007

---

56 Apple, A financial institute relies on smartphones

57 R. Seemann, Corporate reputation management by corporate communications, 2008, page 73

58 W. Griepentrog, Credibility as career factor, January 17, 2011

These retention instruments are such a few of many more tools used to keep the high potentials and their intellectual property in the company. The directors and managers have to ask themselves what they could have done to keep the high potential in order to improve the facts and reasons to keep further high potentials and their intellectual property in their own company.

4.3 CASE STUDY 'HOW TO KEEP INTELLECTUAL PROPERTY IN THE COMPANY'

The following case study shows a fictitious case and a possible solution. At first the author describes a fictitious initial position in order to represent the problems and details of a fictitious company. Afterwards entrepreneurial and strategic objectives are defined. An important component of the case study is the requirements analysis which especially includes the employees. Out of the profiles a concept will be developed. These parts establish the base of the developing phase.

After finishing the developing phase the managers have to create a development and action plan. This plan describes the exact procedure, how to implement the objectives. A regular audit of the results is important. Therefore there should be a continuous improvement process.

The case study closes with a short summary and a conclusion.

a. Initial position

A fictitious international manufacturing company with about 500 employees and 50 million Euro business volumes per year fears that the company will face difficulties with employee retention. Actually the staff turnover rate is alarmingly high compared to other companies in the same business. The company produces exclusive wooden furniture.

The managing director is afraid of losing key positions and A-staff members who posses intellectual property.

Therefore the managing director decides to implement a holistic retention management program in order to identify and keep the employees in key positions and high potentials in the company.

The team which creates the new retention management program consists of the managing director, the director of human resources, two executives of the human resources department and the managers of operation, marketing and administration – if necessary.

The objective is: Especially in the current challenging situation it is essential to identify and keep the high potentials in the own company in order to compete in the highly competitive market in Germany and abroad. Therefore it is the task of the management to create a holistic retention management concept. It is important that the results are company oriented. Expenses and costs have to be within a manageable limit.

b. Entrepreneurial and strategic objectives

The above mentioned team has the task to discuss and define the basic conditions, prerequisites and the objectives. Also it is important to name the task in order to achieve stronger bond to the company – for the time being only for the team members who prepare the program – later for the high potentials.

Results of the entrepreneurial and strategic objectives were:

- An employee survey should elicit the problems and reasons of employee turnover in order to create demand measures.
- The priority analysis is to identify the key positions and high potentials to keep them and their intellectual property in the company.
- There should be different measures for all departments – management, human resources, administration, marketing, production, purchase and sales – to keep the high potentials in the company.
- The focus is on measures which qualify performance oriented employees in order to keep them in the company. There can also be other measures, but the focus should be on qualifying methods.
- The employees should participate as they take part in the survey. The applied measures are based on the statements of the employees.
- A performance review should ensure the effectiveness of the measures. The review differs from department to department because there are different measures to retain the high potentials in the company.

- There should be a cost plan. A set budget enables the control of costs. All expenses and costs have to be within a manageable limit. Therefore the budget for the retention management program is 250.000 Euro which corresponds to 0.5 percent of the business volume.

c. Requirements analysis

At the start of the case study the team has to elicit the problems and reasons of employee turnover. Generally there are some different case studies from consulting companies like Kienbaum, Egon Zehnder, Baumann, etc. But in this case it is very important to know the internal and external problems and reasons for losing employees of this particular company. It is not possible to get the five most common reasons for terminations and find measures against them. It is essential to find the most common – however if possible all – reasons for problems and terminations of employees in the company. Managers cannot implement any measures until they know the real problems and reasons for employee turnover.

There are special questionnaires in order to find out these problems and reasons. Also it is really necessary to answer a questionnaire like this at exit interviews. Often the managers get the most honest answer at this time. But normally it is too late – the employee already has a new job in another company.

<u>Questionnaire for an exit interview</u>

PART I

Date: ________________

Name of employee: ________________ Job title: ________________

Department: ________________ Date joined: ________________

Supervisor: ________________ Date left: ________________

O Termination by employee

O Termination by employer

O Termination agreement Compensation:________________

Further reasons for termination:

____

____

I can imagine working for this company again:

O yes O uncertain O rather no O no

Prerequisites: ____

Questionnaire for an exit interview

PART II

A	**very satisfied**	–	extremely positive, perceived as very good
B	**satisfied**	–	agreed, no objections
C	**improvable**	–	only partially satisfied, could have been better
D	**totally dissatisfied**	–	very unsatisfactory, insufficient

Personal reasons	**YES**		**NO**		**Comments**
Private reason: Family, children					
Education and training					
Career change and reorientation					
Move					
Age and gender					
Journey to work					
Pension					
Other reason(s)					
Operational reasons	**A**	**B**	**C**	**D**	**Comments**
Service of human resources					
Attractiveness of salary and fringe benefits					
Lack of work ethic					
Development and perspectives					
Product and business references					

Lack of challenge					
Application knowhow					
Management policy and style					
Advancement and career track					
Other reason(s)					
Working conditions	**A**	**B**	**C**	**D**	**Comments**
Workplace deficiencies					
Working hours / Flexibility					
Information policy					
Freedom and responsibility					
Health services					
Support and working tools					
Office and office facilities					
Working atmosphere					
Corporate culture					
Supervisor ratio	**A**	**B**	**C**	**D**	**Comments**
Competencies					
Recognition and appreciation					
Authoritarian leadership					
Independence and freedom					
Communication					
Social competencies					
Sympathy and personality					

Dependability					
Other reason(s)					

Table 7: Questionnaire for an exit interview
Source: Own representation, in dependence on: Zeller -Hotel+Restaurant-, Created and implemented by S. Henkel, Exit interviews, 2012

Therefore it is necessary to do appraisal interviews frequently and regularly. Only then it is possible to find out what can be improved to keep the employees in the company. Seldom employees come to the manager to bother. Generally it is only possible in a face to face dialogue between the manager and the employee. Even then the manager needs to take time for the high potential because often they have to feel safe.

Many questions of the questionnaire shown above are very interesting questions for the managers. Many managers are interested in avoiding problems, because it is much easier than extinguishing fires.

The next step to success in the case study is to identify the key positions and the high potentials in one's own company. The employee turnover is connected with some quantifiably and not quantifiably costs. In this regard there is a formula which estimates the costs when an employee leaves which is around 150 percent of an annual salary, often it is more for managers or high potentials.[59] In order to save the costs and keep theses expensive employees in the company it is important to know who these high potentials are.

Firstly the team of the company has to define what a high potential in their company is. A high potential is someone with the ability, aspiration, and commitment to rise and to succeed in more senior, critical positions within the organization. As employees need to have all these three attributes, only a fraction of employees in the top percentile of performance are high potentials.

[59] N. Teltschik, Increased profits with employee participation, 1999, page 125

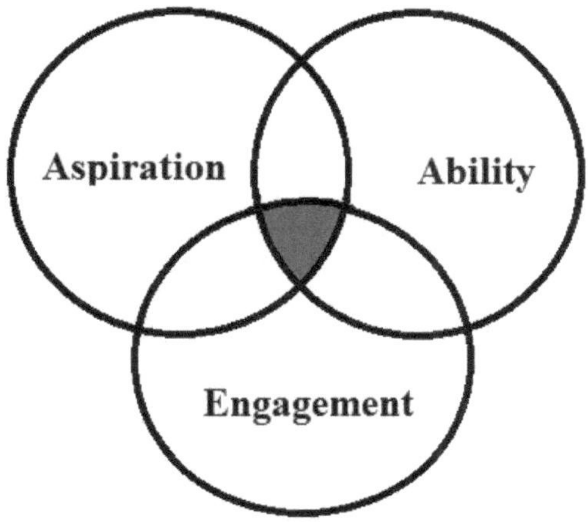

Figure 17: Graphical definition of high potential
Source: Own representation, in dependence on: Corporate leadership council research, High potential employee diagnostic

To narrow the pool of employees, the team should start by identifying high performers and employees in critical roles. To identify high potentials from this employee subset, HR and business leaders should use the diagnostic questions:[60]

- Aspiration questions

  i. Is it important to this individual to rise to a senior management position at his or her organization or another organization?

  ii. Is it important to this individual to receive at least two or more promotions in his or her career?

  iii. Is it important to this individual to be recognized as an expert in his or her field by people in and outside of the organization?

  iv. Is it important to this individual to receive greater and greater amounts of responsibility over the course of his or her career?

  v. Is it important to this individual to receive large increases in financial compensation over the course of his or her career?

- Ability questions
  - i. Does this individual gather information from all available sources before drawing conclusions?
  - ii. Can this individual logically piece together a solution to a problem?
  - iii. Does this individual absorb complex concepts and incorporate them into his or her work?
  - iv. Can this individual effectively manage difficult employees and inspire others?
  - v. Does this individual remain calm under pressure at work?
- Commitment questions
  - i. Is this individual proud to work for the organization?
  - ii. Does this individual speak highly of the organization when speaking to others?
  - iii. Does the organization have a great deal of personal meaning for this individual?
  - iv. Does this individual believe that the best way to advance in his or her career is to stay with the organization?
  - v. Does this individual frequently try to help others who have heavy workloads?

By using this analysis it is possible to select and name the key positions in the company and to identify the high potentials.

d. Concept development

The concept especially includes different measures for all departments with focus on qualifying methods. All employees of the company should take part in the survey in order to develop the right and most effective retention instruments.

---

[60] Corporate leadership council research, High potential employee diagnostic

The result is as follows: All retention instruments which are pointed out in chapter 4 have been implemented in the company. Further more there is a special bonus for each department:

- Management

  The team decides to implement a profit sharing tool for the management. It is a powerful tool in promoting financial security for the company. The top managers benefit from their decisions. They get more money for right decisions and no money for bad decisions.

- Human resources / Administration / Marketing / Purchase

  These four departments are united to one bonus and retention tool because all employees of these departments work inhouse. Also it is the same way to evaluate their performances.

  For these four departments a performance oriented tool has been developed. As soon as the targets – which are created in appraisal interviews – are reached by an employee, he / she will receive a bonus. The bonuses are staggered for each milestone. The more milestones are reached the more bonuses are paid.

- Production

  Even for the production department there is a performance oriented bonus tool. It depends on the quantity but also on the quality of the products.

- Sales

  The sales department will receive commissions for each sold product. It depends also on the quantity of sold products. The more customers are buying the products of the company the more commission will be paid.

All the retention tools and the benefit tools are selected by the employees. A survey among the employees shows that these are tool which are desired by the employees.

e. Development and action planning

Measures in departments	Times Start date: July 2013	Costs
Management	December 2013	35.000 Euro
Human resources	October 2013	15.000 Euro
Administration	October 2013	15.000 Euro
Marketing	October 2013	15.000 Euro
Production	September 2013	75.000 Euro
Purchase	October 2013	15.000 Euro
Sales	November 2013	80.000 Euro
	Implementation start: January 2013	**250.000 Euro**

Table 8: Development and action planning, case study II

Source: Own representation

f. Measurement of results

The team also implements a continuous improvement process which should check the results regularly. Following cycle is created by the team:

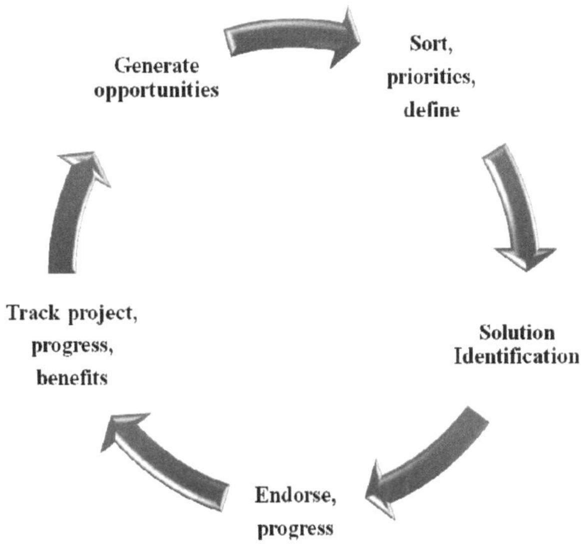

Figure 18: Cycle of continuous improvement process
Source: Own representation, in dependence on: M. Lovett, Good enough never is, September 06, 2010

g. Conclusion of case study

This case study should be an instruction for directors and managers to keep high potentials in their own company. Primarily the case study should show the various retention tools and sensitize managers to use it.

Also the aim of the case study is to clarify that it is positive for the company to keep the best employees in one's own company. There is the fact of intellectual property which has already been discussed. But there are also things like employees' development, employees' qualifications, company's business development, products' quality, etc.

Generally you have a lot of advantages when you develop and implement a retention management program. Of course, there are also employees who do not meet the requirements of the company. These employees are the B-staff and C-staff members. The company has to try to invest in B-staff members in order to turn them into A-staff members and to get rid of C-staff members.

The easiest way for the company to be a successful company is to have a high rate of A-staff members – the easiest way for an employee to make career is to be or to become an A-staff members – *so why are we not all A-staff members?*[61]

---

[61] S. Henkel, A question which has to be discussed, emerged from the Master-Thesis "Identification and motivation of high potentials to keep their intellectual property in the company", 2013

5 CONCLUSION

More and more managers realize that it is one of the most important management tasks to identify and motivate the high potentials and to keep their intellectual property in the company. It costs not only too much money for the company to lose the A-staff members, because the human resources department has to recruit anew and develop them. Even there are the costs which cannot be calculated. Whenever a high potential switches to another company he / she will transfer the intellectual property. That could be a chance for the new company and a big risk for the current company. Property which is only in the employees' brain will be lost. Perhaps it is possible for the switching employee to implement the holistic knowledge in the new company – then it is doubly hard. Not only that the company loses a high potential, the company runs the risk of getting a new competitor. Many managers realize the big loss of the company – a high potential and his / her intellectual property.

In this chapter this Master-Thesis shows how to identify the A-staff, B-staff and C-staff members of the company. For the managers it is very important to know which employee is in which group. Only then it is possible for the managers to develop them to a high potential. The second chapter shows how motivation works. Most managers know the different monetary and non-monetary motivation tools. Therefore in this chapter the author describes how lack of motivation is caused. In order to motivate an employee the managers have to know the reasons for the lack of motivation. This chapter closes with a case study how to motivate high potentials. The third chapter shows some retention instruments which are already used by a few companies. The goal is to sensitize all the managers to this very important topic in order to keep high potentials in the company and enable the employees to job satisfaction. Also this chapter close with a case study about how to keep the high potentials and their intellectual property in one's own company.

As already mentioned the goal of the Master-Thesis is it to sensitize directors and managers to this topic. Unfortunately there are also a few companies which are using retention programs in order to keep their high potentials. Often there are attempts to implement such a program but it is not as easy as it sounds. The manger and the program team need a lot of time to develop a program which is particularly suitable for one's own company. After the development, the next step is to implement it. The implementation often needs much more time than the development. Small and medium-sized companies often do not have the time for creating an own retention program. For bigger companies it is easier because they have their own human resources department which can build a team with the managers of each department in order to create, develop and implement a retention program which motivates all the employees. This helps to keep the high potentials – and also the B-staff members – in the company.

This Master-Thesis, especially the case studies answer two further questions which should be solved in the future by economic sciences.

Case study I: The easiest way for the company to be a successful company is to have a high rate of motivated employees – the easiest way for an employee to be motivated is to be open minded in appraisal interviews and management by objectives – *so how is it possible to have companies without these motivation tools?*

Case Study II: The easiest way for the company to be a successful company is to have a high rate of A-staff members – the easiest way for an employee to make career is to be or to become an A-staff member – *so why are we not all A-staff members?*

In order to answer these two scientific questions, the analysis has to go on. It is an exciting topic which captures more and more attention. Therefore the author tries to answer open questions in further documents.

It is a practical consequence of this Master-Thesis to find time to create, develop and implement retention and motivation programs also in small and medium-sized companies and in all big companies which have not got such instruments and tools yet. The practical value of this Master-Thesis is to give an instruction how to identify and motivate high potentials in order to keep their intellectual property in one's own company.

III. BIBLIOGRAPHY

The author used the following bibliography for this Master-Thesis. In order to have a better overview, the bibliography is divided into books, business studies, companies, universities and business leaders.

a. Books

Adams D., Dirk Gently's holistic detective agency, Ullstein publishing house, 7th edition, 1994

Bohlander G.-W., Snell S.-A. Snell, Managing human resources, South-Western Cengage Learning publishing house, Mason, 2010

Breisig T., performance appraisal, Bund publishing house, 2003

Bullinger H.-J., Warnecke H.-J., Westkämper E., New organization forms in companies, Springer publishing house, Berlin, Heidelberg, New York, 2nd edition, 2003

Drucker P.F., Management, Allied publishing house, London, 3rd edition, 1975

Drumm H.-J., Human resources, Springer publishing house, Berlin, Heidelberg, 6th edition, 2008

Fulmer R.-M., Bleak J.-L., The leadership advantage, AMACOM publishing house, New York, 2008

Gitman L.-J., McDaniel C., The future of business, Thomson South-Western publishing house, Mason, 2008

Herzberg F., Mausner B., Snyderman B.-B., Motivation to work, Transaction publishing house, New Brunswick, 12th edition, 2009

Janssen H., Recruit, develop and keep the best employees, Praxium publishing house, Zürich, 11th edition, 2011

Jossey-Bass, Team bulding, Fourth edition, John Wiley publishing house, New York, 2007

Kasper H., Mayrhofer W., Personality management, leadership and organization, Linde publishing house, 3rd edition, 2002

Kirchler E., Industrial and organizational psychology, Facultas publishing house, Wien, 2nd edition, 2008

Knoblauch J., Kurz J., To find and keep the best employees, Campus publishing house, Frankfurt/Main, 2nd edition, 2009

Liebhart, C., Employee retention management and action errors, Druck Diplomica publishing house, Hamburg, 2009

Maslow A.-H., Maslow on management, John Wiley publishing house, New York, revised edition, 1998

McClelland D.-C., Human motivation, Press Syndicate of University of Cambridge, Cambridge, 1987

Müller R., Systematic performance appraisal and management by objectives, Praxium publishing house, Zürich, 2005

Mosley R., Employer brand, Shoulders of giants publishing house, 2009

Odgers, P., Administrative office management, South-Western publishing house, Mason, 2005

Paff D., Understanding, winning and inspiring costumers, Campus publishing house, Frankfurt/Main, 2006

Rodriguez R., Latino talent, Effective strategies to recruit, retain and develop Hispanic professionals, John Wiley publishing house, New Jersey, 2008

Ryan R.-M., Deci E.-L., Intrinsic and extrinsic motivation, Plenum publishing house, New York, 1985

Schroeder R.-G., Flynn B.-B., High performance manufacturing, John Wiley publishing house, New York, 2001

Seemann, R., Corporate reputation management by corporate communication, Cuviller publishing house, Göttingen, 2008

Svenson O., Maule A.J., Time pressure and stress in human judgment and decision making, Plenum publishing house, New York, 1993

Teltschik H., Increased profits with employee participation, Lang publishing house, Frankfurt/Main, illustrated edition, 1999

Tomczak T., Kernstock J., Esch F.-R., Hermann An., Behavioral branding, Gabler publishing house, Wiesbaden, 3rd edition, 2012

Young, I., Mental models, Rosenfeld media publishing house, 2011

b. Business studies

Die Welt, 1.800 percent more sick days on the basis of burnouts, January 27, 2013

Handelsblatt, Lack of motivation costs companies billions, March 06, 2013

Harvard Business Manager, Persuading properly, December 22, 2011

PricewaterhouseCoopers, Strategies in the war of talents, April, 2011

PricewaterhouseCoopers, The future of work in 2020, May 2010

Service value, Recognition and appreciation, September 18, 2012

c. Companies

Apple, A financial institute relies on smartphones

Beckhäuser Staff & Solutions, nobisCum, A study of employee satisfaction

BKK health insurance, 1.800 percent more sick days on the basis of burnouts, 2013

Centre for European Economic Research, Specific measures for older employees and late career employment, March 14, 2013

Corporate leadership council research, High potential employee diagnostic

Gallup, One in four employees has noticed internally, 2011

Google, Life at Google

IHK Nordwestfalen, Guide for assessment and appraisal interview

IHK Potsdam, ABC analysis of employees

Institute of German economy Cologne, Extras for good performance, August 2010

Institute of German economy Cologne, Hire and fire is out, 2010

Keller Consulting, Motivation, March 01, 2013

Konsensus-analysis Asklepios, Annual report, 2012

OECD, Work life balance

PennState, Redmond B.-R., Herzberg's two factor theory, November 11, 2012

T. Johnson & Associates, September 11, 2011

Xinnovations e.V., Manager to staff, January 10, 2012

ZELLER -Hotel+Restaurant-, Exit interviews, 2012

d. Universities

Technical university Cottbus, Our claim

University St. Gallen, Prof. Dr. R. Wunderer, The foursome classification, 1997-1999

e. Business leaders

Collins J., Summary: Good to great, November 01, 2011

Clegg S.-J., 360 degree feedback, 2009

Finkelstein, J., Maslow's hierarchy of needs, October 27, 2006

Griepentrog W., Credibility as career factor, January 17, 2011

Johnson R., China has found a brutally simple way to steal corporate secrets, February 19, 2013

Lovett M., Good enough never is, September 06, 2010

Niebuhr R., Influential American theologian, philosopher and political scientist, 1941

Patel N., How to keep your employees happy while pushing them to their limits, May 18, 2011

Petermann Dipl.-Ing. J., Weblog easy and personal, February 17, 2007

Schröder, Dr. W., Personnel systems, November 02, 2011

Voser P., Chief Financial Officer of Royal Dutch Shell, 2004-2009

Walker B., Extreme personalities in teams, Annual meeting of the academy of management, 2011

Warren, N., The big five personality test

Welch J., General Manager of General Electric, 1981-2001

IV. APPENDIX / LIST OF LAYOUTS

BKK-Krankenkasse

Abo Shop TV-Programm Wetter Anmelden Registrieren

zur Startseite machen

Suchen

Home Politik Wirtschaft Geld Sport Wissen Panorama Kultur Reise Motor Regionales Meinung Videos Marktplatz

IN DEN NACHRICHTEN: Amanda Knox | Boris Beresowski | Zypern | D-Mark | Nordkorea 28. Mrz. 2013, 10:59

Home › Wirtschaft › 1800 Prozent mehr Krankentage durch Burn-out

Lesen Sie WELT DIGITAL Komplett und sichern Sie sich ein iPad mini. Nur bis 31.03.2013 › Jetzt bestellen

27.01.13 | Gesundheit

1800 Prozent mehr Krankentage durch Burn-out

Von 2004 bis 2011 sind die Krankheitstage wegen Burn-out um das 18-Fache gestiegen. Gewerkschaften und Arbeitgeber wollen dagegen vorgehen, aber sie streiten noch über die Ursachen.

Von Ileana Grabitz und Flora Wisdorff

ARTIKEL EMPFEHLEN

207 59 23

E-Mail Empfehlen Twittern +1

Kommentare (136) Drucken

— PSYCHISCHE ERKRANKUNGEN AUF DEM VORMARSCH —

Krankheitstage durch das Burn-out-Syndrom 2004 bis 2011
je 1000 BKK-Mitglieder, ohne Rentner

Gesamt Frauen Männer

...

URL: http://www.welt.de/wirtschaft/article113159916/1800-Prozent-mehr-Krankentage-durch-Burn-out.html, visited on March 28, 2013

Handelsblatt Finanzen Unternehmen Politik Technologie Auto Meinung Sport Panorama

Industrie Banken Versicherungen Handel + Dienstleister IT + Medien Mittelstand Management Beruf + Büro

ARTIKEL KOMMENTARE (1) DOSSIERS

GALLUP-STUDIE 06.03.2013, 16:57 Uhr

Fehlende Motivation kostet Firmen Milliarden

Wenn Angestellte keinen Spaß mehr an der Arbeit haben, liegt das meist an den direkten Vorgesetzten. Das zumindest zeigt eine neue Studie. Vor allem Ältere fühlen sich vom Chef vernachlässigt. Das kostet Milliarden.

URL: http://www.handelsblatt.com/unternehmen/management/strategie/gallup-studie-fehlende-motivation-kostet-firmen-milliarden/7888974.html, visited on March 28, 2013

Harvard Business manager

DAS WISSEN DER BESTEN

HOME TRENDS STRATEGIEN MEINUNGEN BLOGS

Home > Meinungen

22.03.2012 Text

drucken verschicken bookmarken

Selbstmanagement

In 30 Sekunden überzeugen

Von Ron Ashkenas

Wenn Sie andere für sich gewinnen möchten, ist der erste Eindruck meist entscheidend. Lernen Sie von der TV-Werbung, wie Sie Aufmerksamkeit auf sich lenken, klare Botschaften vermitteln und positiv in Erinnnerung bleiben.

In der Halbzeit großer Sportergeignisse wie etwa dem Super-Bowl, dem Finale der US-amerikanischen Football-Profiliga, zeigt sich wie stark ein nur 30 Sekunden langer Werbespots das Image eines Unternehmens beeinflussen kann. Aber wie oft arbeiten wir an

URL: http://www.harvardbusinessmanager.de/meinungen/artikel/a-822578.html, visited on March 28, 2013

pwc

Deutschland

Deutsch | English

Home Im Fokus Branchen & Märkte Dienstleistungen Veranstaltungen Wir über uns Presse

Consulting
Energiewende
Finanzierung
Governance & Compliance
Internationalisierung
Nachhaltigkeit
Personal
Prozessoptimierung
Rechnungslegung
Risikomanagement
Steuerberatung
Transaktionen

Strategien im Kampf um die besten Köpfe

Der "War of Talent" wurde bereits vor zehn Jahren ausgerufen. Gewonnen haben ihn die meisten Unternehmen noch nicht. Im Gegenteil: Zwei Drittel der Vorstandeschefs weltweit, die PwC für den CEO Survey befragt hat, beklagen: Sie finden nicht genügend qualifizierte Arbeitskräfte, um ihre Geschäftsstrategie umzusetzen. Besonders in den Schwellenländern, wo sie verstärkt wachsen wollen, fehlt es an geeigneten Talenten. Logische Konsequenz: 92 Prozent der deutschen CEOs wollen ihre Talentmanagement-Strategie verändern. Welche Strategien Erfolg versprechen, analysiert Till Lohmann, PwC-Experte für Personalmanagement.

Download

Der CEO Survey zeigt, dass Vorstandschefs auf der ganzen Welt sehr optimistisch in die Zukunft blicken. Die positiven Wachstumsprognosen spiegeln sich auch in der Personalpolitik wider: 62 Prozent der deutschen Vorstandschefs wollen die Anzahl ihrer Mitarbeiter in den kommenden zwölf Monaten erhöhen. Das sind mehr als im globalen Vergleich: Weltweit planen immerhin gut die Hälfte der Unternehmenschefs, mehr Mitarbeiter einzustellen. Besonders die klassischen Industrie-

URL: http://www.pwc.de/de/prozessoptimierung/strategien-im-kampf-um-die-besten-koepfe.jhtml, visited on March 28, 2013

pwc

Deutschland

Deutsch | English

Home | Im Fokus | Branchen & Märkte | Dienstleistungen | Veranstaltungen | Wir über uns | Presse

- Consulting
- Energiewende
- Finanzierung
- Governance & Compliance
- Internationalisierung
- Nachhaltigkeit
- Personal
- Prozessoptimierung ▸
- Rechnungslegung
- Risikomanagement
- Steuerberatung
- Transaktionen

Die Zukunft der Arbeit im Jahr 2020

Worauf legen Mitarbeiter bei der Wahl ihres Arbeitgebers Wert? Wie gelingt es Unternehmen, ihre besten Kräfte zu halten und an die Firma zu binden? Um Antworten auf diese Fragen ging es bei der internationalen Befragung "Managing tomorrow's people: Future of work" von PwC. Ein wichtiges Ergebnis: Unternehmen, die von ihren Mitarbeitern dauerhaft zu viel erwarten, müssen mit einer Abwanderung rechnen – sodass in Zeiten des Aufschwungs Schlüsselkräfte fehlen könnten.

Wo sehen Sie sich im Jahr 2020? Das ist die zentrale Frage der Befragung aus der Serie "Managing Tomorrow's People". Rund 5.700 Mitarbeiter aus 113 Ländern haben Anfang 2010 ihre Antwort darauf gegeben. Unternehmen können aus den Ergebnissen wichtige Schlüsse für ihr Personalmanagement ziehen.

Mehr Verantwortung, mehr Geld

In zehn Jahren sehen sich 44 Prozent der Befragten in einer Position mit mehr Verantwortung und einem entsprechend höheren Gehalt. 36 Prozent hoffen darauf, dass sie in der kommenden Dekade ein ausgewogeneres Verhältnis zwischen Arbeit und Privatleben haben werden. Und 20 Prozent möchten ihr eigener Chef sein, sehen sich als Selbstständige.

URL: http://www.pwc.de/de/prozessoptimierung/die-zukunft-der-arbeit-im-jahr-2020.jhtml, visited on March 28, 2013

ServiceValue

Home

Unternehmen
Leistungen
Referenzen

Magazin

18.09.2012

Stress am Arbeitsplatz: Die Ressource Zeit ist begrenzt

Immer mehr leisten in immer weniger Zeit, das geht auf Dauer nicht gut. Der Umgang mit der Ressource Zeit ist nicht nur eine private Herausforderung. Im „Freizeit Monitor 2011" des Instituts für Zukunftsfragen beklagen die Bürger zu wenig Zeit für Privates. In unserer aktuellen Arbeitnehmer-Studie wird die Zeitknappheit sogar als Belastungsfaktor Nummer 1 genannt. Zum ungesunden Stressfaktor wird sie vor allem dann, wenn zu hohe Zielerwartungen und fehlender Entscheidungsspielraum mit einhergehen.

URL: http://www.servicevalue.de/magazin/artikel/stress-am-arbeitsplatz-die-ressource-zeit-ist-begrenzt/, visited on March 28, 2013

Grupo BBVA

Eine Bank setzt auf iPhone und iPad.

Die Grupo BBVA ist eines der weltweit größten Finanzinstitute. BBVA setzt auf iPhone und iPad, um wichtige Abläufe zu beschleunigen, die interne Kommunikation zu verbessern und seinen 49,8 Millionen Kunden auf der ganzen Welt den bestmöglichen Service zu bieten.

„Wir stellen fest, dass sich die Produktivität allein durch die Tatsache erhöht, dass ein Mitarbeiter ein iPhone oder iPad hat. Die Menschen arbeiten damit einfach anders", sagt Luis Uguina, der bei der BBVA für die Remote Channels und neue digitale Geschäftsfelder verantwortlich ist.

Mit iPad und iPhone kann das Management schneller und effizienter geschäftliche Entscheidungen treffen und Probleme lösen. Auch wenn Manager auf Geschäftsreise sind oder gerade in einer Besprechung stecken, können sie schnell Spesenabrechnungen bewilligen oder auf dringende Anfragen reagieren. „Vorgänge, die früher Wochen dauerten, sind jetzt in wenigen Stunden abgeschlossen", so Uguina. „Die Leute können jetzt unterwegs Aufgaben erledigen, die früher nur an einem Computer möglich waren."

Und die Entscheidung für iPhone und iPad ist auch besonders sinnvoll, wenn man berücksichtigt, dass sich die Grupo BBVA verstärkt hin zu cloudbasierten, auf Teamwork ausgelegten Abläufen orientiert. Denn die Geräte helfen dabei, mühelos auf Firmendaten zuzugreifen und Kollegen zu kontaktieren.

Unternehmensprofil

- Gegründet 1857 im spanischen Bilbao
- 110.000 Mitarbeiter in 32 Ländern
- Mehr als 49 Millionen Kunden
- Über 7.400 Filialen in Spanien und Lateinamerika sowie ein wachsender Marktanteil in den USA
- www.bbva.com

URL: http://www.apple.com/de/ipad/business/profiles/bbva/, visited on March 28, 2013

BECKHÄUSER®
PERSONAL&LÖSUNGEN

Sedanstraße 27
97082 Würzburg

Fon: +49 (0)9 31 – 4 52 89 90
Fax: +49 (0)9 31 – 4 52 89 91

E-Mail: info@beckhaeuser.com
Web: www.beckhaeuser.com

nobisCum®

Sedanstraße 23 b
97082 Würzburg

Fon: +49 (0)9 31 – 7 96 67 0
Fax: +49 (0)9 31 – 7 96 67 29

E-Mail: info@nobisCum.de
Web: www.nobisCum.de

Eine Studie zur Mitarbeiterzufriedenheit

URL: http://www.brand-ladenbau.de/upload/dokumente/10013.pdf, visited on March 28, 2013

| Veranstaltungen | Weiterbildung

Kontakt | Presse | Seite drucken

ZEW
Zentrum für Europäische Wirtschaftsforschung GmbH
Centre for European Economic Research

Pressemitteilung

13.03.2013 – ZEW (jfr/ggr)
Schlagworte: **Arbeitskräfte**, **Ältere Arbeitskräfte**

» Artikel empfehlen: E-Mail | Social Media
» Feedback an die Pressestelle senden

Ältere Arbeitnehmer - Längerer Verbleib in Unternehmen mit altersgemischten Arbeitsteams

Eine altersgerechte Ausstattung des Arbeitsplatzes, verringerte Arbeitszeiten und Leistungsanforderungen, altersgemischte Arbeitsteams, allgemeine Weiterbildung, spezielle Weiterbildung sowie Altersteilzeit: Unternehmen setzen vor dem Hintergrund der demografischen Alterung und dem sich abzeichnenden Fachkräftemangel immer häufiger auf eine oder mehrere dieser Maßnahmen, um ältere Arbeitnehmer länger an sich zu binden. Eine Studie des Zentrums für Europäische Wirtschaftsforschung (ZEW), Mannheim, hat diese Maßnahmen nun erstmals auf den Prüfstand gestellt. Es zeigt sich, dass nur altersgemischte Teams die gewünschte längere Beschäftigungsdauer zur Folge haben. Dagegen scheint Altersteilzeit die Beschäftigungsdauer älterer Arbeitnehmer eher zu verringern und alle anderen der vorab aufgelisteten Maßnahmen beeinflussen die Entscheidung, wie lange ältere Arbeitnehmer im Unternehmen verbleiben, überhaupt nicht.

Für seine Analyse verwendet das ZEW Längsschnittsdaten des Instituts für Arbeitsmarkt- und Berufsforschung (IAB) zu älteren Arbeitnehmern zwischen 40 und 65 Jahren aus dem Jahr 2002. Dabei werden 1.063 westdeutsche Unternehmen betrachtet, die mindestens fünf ältere Mitarbeiter beschäftigen. Ostdeutsche Unternehmen werden nicht berücksichtigt, da für sie keine Daten für den Zeitraum vor 1990 vorliegen.

URL: http://www.zew.de/de/presse/2258/aeltere-arbeitnehmer---laengerer-verbleib-in-unternehmen-mit-altersgemischten-arbeitsteams, visited on March 28, 2013

HR Leadership Council™

High-Potential Employee Diagnostic

Purpose of this Diagnostic: A high-potential employee is someone with the ability, aspiration, and engagement to rise and to succeed in more senior, critical positions within the organization. Because employees need all three attributes, only a fraction of employees in the top percentile of performance are high-potential. This diagnostic will help you identify those employees who have all three attributes.

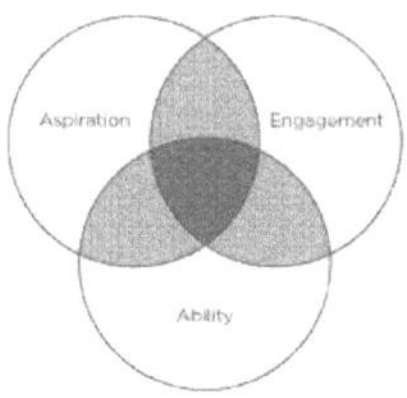

How to Use this Diagnostic: To narrow the pool of employees, HR should start by identifying high performers and employees in critical roles. To identify high-potential employees from this employee subset, HR and business leaders should use the diagnostic questions on the next tab. The ability questions may be best answered by the individual's manager and the aspiration and engagement questions may be best answered by the individual.

Please ensure your calculation options are set to 'Automatic' so the High-Potential Employee Diagnostic will work properly.

For More Information: These questions are a sub-set of those available in the Corporate Leadership Council's HIPO Identification Diagnostic tool. For more information on the full tool, please contact the Corporate Leadership Council.

URL:http://www.google.de/url?sa=t&rct=j&q=&esrc=s&source=web&cd=1&ved=0CDUQFjAA&url=http%3A%2F%2Fwww.executiveboard.com%2Fexbd-resources%2Fpdf%2Fhuman-resources%2Fsmb-hr%2Fhigh-potential-employee-diagnos-tic.xls&ei=MyZUUc2lK6T64QSUpoDYDA&usg=AFQjCNHSu6Mjzcxub27zovzPHrAtjSVI2Q&sig2=F64T8j9HCr5HeXUhc47_SA&bvm=bv.44342787,d.bGE, visited on March 28, 2013

online impulse
DAS MAGAZIN FÜR UNTERNEHMER

Suchbegri

Nachrichten | Wissen | Rechner & Daten | Marktplatz

Schlagzeilen | Unternehmen | › Management | Gründer | Finanzen + Vorsorge | Recht + Steuer

0 BEWERTUNGEN

EMPFEHLEN Share

06.03.2013

Gallup-Index

Jeder vierte Arbeitnehmer hat innerlich gekündigt

Von: Bernd Röder

Rund 8,4 Millionen Menschen in Deutschland fühlen einer Studie zufolge keine emotionale Bindung zu ihrem Unternehmen. Vor allem ältere Arbeitnehmer verlieren demnach die Lust am Job. Das kostet die Wirtschaft Milliarden.

URL: http://www.impulse.de/management/:Gallup-Index--Jeder-vierte-Arbeitnehmer-hat-innerlich-gekuendigt/1033567.html, visited on March 28, 2013

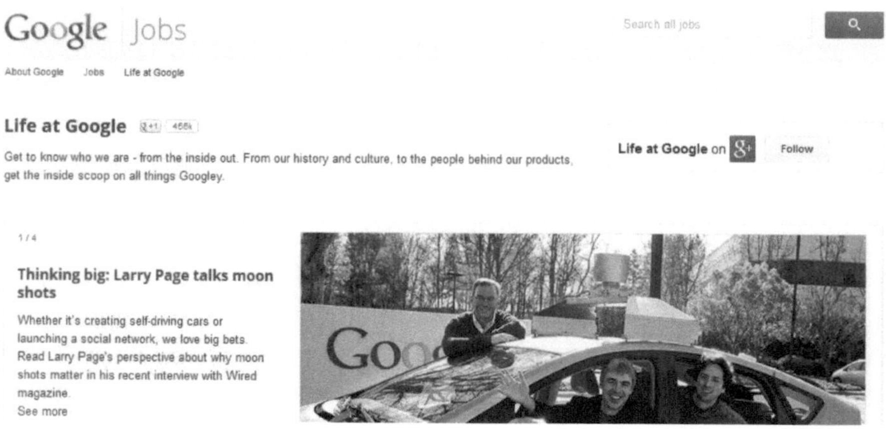

Google Jobs

Search all jobs

About Google Jobs Life at Google

Life at Google

Get to know who we are - from the inside out. From our history and culture, to the people behind our products, get the inside scoop on all things Googley.

Life at Google on Follow

1 / 4

Thinking big: Larry Page talks moon shots

Whether it's creating self-driving cars or launching a social network, we love big bets. Read Larry Page's perspective about why moon shots matter in his recent interview with Wired magazine.

See more

URL: http://www.google.com/about/jobs/lifeatgoogle/, visited on March 28, 2013

Leitfaden Beurteilung und Beurteilungsgespräch

Inhalt

(Mit Klick auf die Überschriften können Sie direkt zu den einzelnen Absätzen springen)

URL:http://www.ihk-nordwestfalen.de/fileadmin/medien/02_Wirtschaft/22_Aus-_und_Weiterbildung/00_Ausbildungsbetriebe/Ausbildungsberatung/Zeugnis/leitfaden_beurteilung.pdf, visited on March 28, 2013

A-B-C-Analyse der Mitarbeiter

1. Das Problem

Viele Unternehmer und Führungskräfte sind mit ihren Mitarbeitern unzufrieden. Innerhalb des Mitarbeiterkreises ergeben sich Spannungen, weil große Unterschiede bezüglich der fachlichen Fitness sowie in der Motivation der Mitarbeiter vorhanden sind.

Welche Mitarbeiter die Richtigen sind, um

2. Die Ziele und der Nutzen

Lernen Sie zu ermitteln, welche Ihrer Mitarbeiter zu den »Stützen des Unternehmens« gehören.

Unterscheiden Sie bei Mitarbeitern mit Leistungsschwächen diejenigen, die der fachlichen und der persönlichen Unterstützung bedürfen, von denjenigen, die »Dienst nach Vorschrift« machen oder im Inneren bereits gekündigt haben.

Diese Methode hilft Ihnen, statt eines allgemeinen »Bauchgefühles« konkrete Hilfen zur Hand zu haben, um die verschiedenen Mitarbeiter in ihrer Weiterentwicklung zu unterstützen.

URL:http://www.potsdam.ihk24.de/linkableblob/1378462/data/Forum_1_Beitrag_Rainer_Westphal-data.pdf, visited on March 28, 2013

Institut der deutschen Wirtschaft Köln

Sitemap | Newslette

Themen
Wissenschaft
Infodienste
iwd
Archiv
Redaktion
Sachregister
IW-Nachrichten
IW-Dossiers
Argumente zu Unternehmensfragen
Umwelt-Service
Immobilien-Monitor
Gewerkschaftsspiegel
Wirtschaft und Ethik
Newsletter (in Englisch)

Home > Infodienste > iwd > Archiv

Variable Vergütung

Extras für gute Arbeit

Drei Viertel der deutschen Arbeitnehmer befürworten eine leistungsgemäße Bezahlung. Die Unternehmen bieten beim Gehalt verschiedene Varianten an: sowohl erfolgsorientierte Boni wie auch Leistungsprämien oder variable Vergütungsbestandteile.

Nach einer aktuellen Befragung von über 1.800 Unternehmen durch das Institut der deutschen Wirtschaft Köln (IW) verknüpfen fast vier von zehn Unternehmen Prämien mit Zielen, die erreicht werden sollen. Mehr als die Hälfte der befragten Firmen will mit dieser leistungsorientierten Vergütung ihre Mitarbeiter an das Unternehmen binden (Grafik).

Auch eine Studie der Unternehmensberatung Hay Group bestätigt die IW-Ergebnisse: Danach halten 85 Prozent der befragten Betriebe es für sinnvoll, die Ziele und Leistungen des Topmanagements sowie der leitenden Angestellten mit einer variablen Vergütungskomponente zu verknüpfen.

URL: http://www.iwkoeln.de/de/infodienste/iwd/archiv/beitrag/27533, visited on March 28, 2013

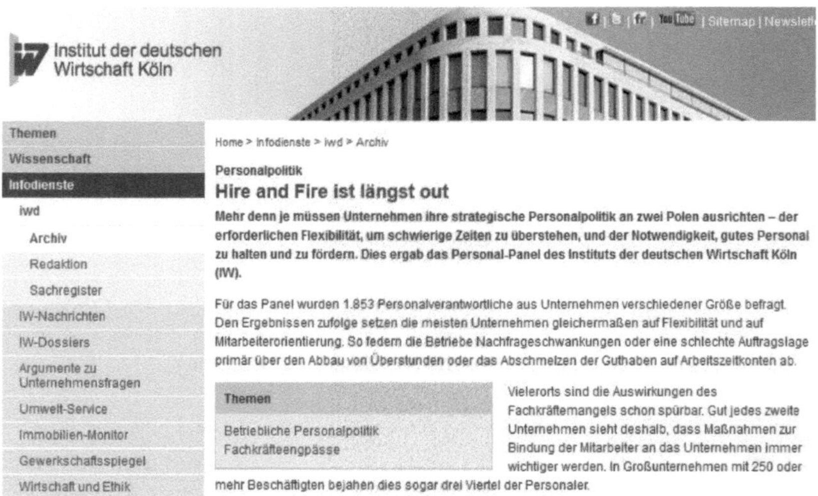

Institut der deutschen Wirtschaft Köln

Sitemap | Newslett

Themen
Wissenschaft
Infodienste
iwd
Archiv
Redaktion
Sachregister
IW-Nachrichten
IW-Dossiers
Argumente zu Unternehmensfragen
Umwelt-Service
Immobilien-Monitor
Gewerkschaftsspiegel
Wirtschaft und Ethik

Home > Infodienste > iwd > Archiv

Personalpolitik

Hire and Fire ist längst out

Mehr denn je müssen Unternehmen ihre strategische Personalpolitik an zwei Polen ausrichten – der erforderlichen Flexibilität, um schwierige Zeiten zu überstehen, und der Notwendigkeit, gutes Personal zu halten und zu fördern. Dies ergab das Personal-Panel des Instituts der deutschen Wirtschaft Köln (IW).

Für das Panel wurden 1.853 Personalverantwortliche aus Unternehmen verschiedener Größe befragt. Den Ergebnissen zufolge setzen die meisten Unternehmen gleichermaßen auf Flexibilität und auf Mitarbeiterorientierung. So federn die Betriebe Nachfrageschwankungen oder eine schlechte Auftragslage primär über den Abbau von Überstunden oder das Abschmelzen der Guthaben auf Arbeitszeitkonten ab.

Themen
Betriebliche Personalpolitik
Fachkräfteengpässe

Vielerorts sind die Auswirkungen des Fachkräftemangels schon spürbar. Gut jedes zweite Unternehmen sieht deshalb, dass Maßnahmen zur Bindung der Mitarbeiter an das Unternehmen immer wichtiger werden. In Großunternehmen mit 250 oder mehr Beschäftigten bejahen dies sogar drei Viertel der Personaler.

URL: http://www.iwkoeln.de/de/infodienste/iwd/archiv/beitrag/27847, visited on March 28, 2013

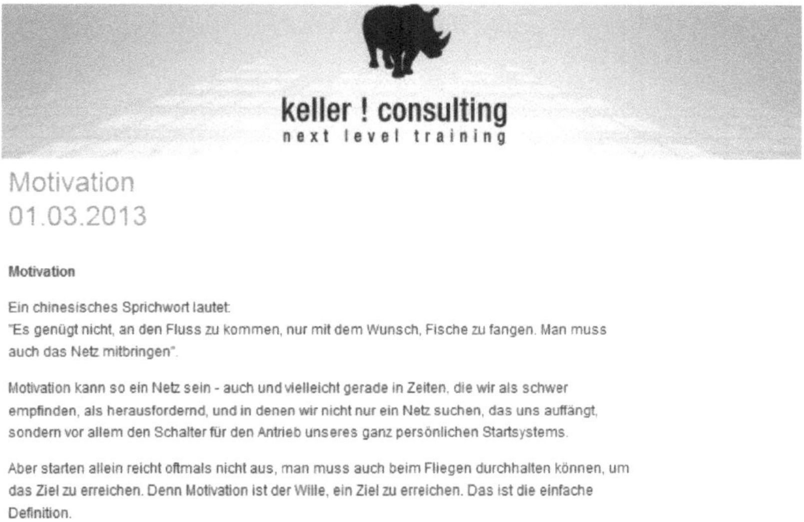
keller ! consulting
next level training

Motivation
01.03.2013

Motivation

Ein chinesisches Sprichwort lautet:
"Es genügt nicht, an den Fluss zu kommen, nur mit dem Wunsch, Fische zu fangen. Man muss auch das Netz mitbringen".

Motivation kann so ein Netz sein - auch und vielleicht gerade in Zeiten, die wir als schwer empfinden, als herausfordernd, und in denen wir nicht nur ein Netz suchen, das uns auffängt, sondern vor allem den Schalter für den Antrieb unseres ganz persönlichen Startsystems.

Aber starten allein reicht oftmals nicht aus, man muss auch beim Fliegen durchhalten können, um das Ziel zu erreichen. Denn Motivation ist der Wille, ein Ziel zu erreichen. Das ist die einfache Definition.

URL: http://www.kellerconsulting.de/unser-angebot/fuer-jedermann/motivation.html, visited on March 28,

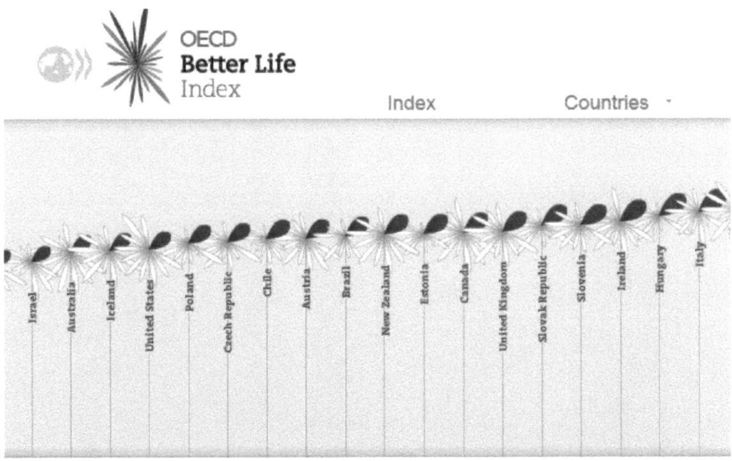

2013

Work-Life Balance

URL: http://www.oecdbetterlifeindex.org/topics/work-life-balance/, visited on March 28, 2013

PENNSTATE **Fall 2012 Job design case** Extras

1 Hinzugefügt von BRIAN FRANCIS REDMOND, zuletzt bearbeitet von ckl5049@psu.edu am Nov 11, 2012 (Änderung anzeigen) Kommentar einblenden

Introduction

Job design is the process of making a job more appealing (or desirable) to increase motivation. Although not without skeptics and controversy, for more than fifty years theories and research have supported the idea that those who find work meaningful, challenging, and interesting are more engaged and productive (PSU, 2012, Lesson 10, p. 2). Two rather prominent theories will be examined here. The first, Herzberg's Two-Factor Theory, was a trailblazer of sorts. Herzberg's two factors were extrinsic aspects of the job such as pay and benefits and intrinsic factors like feeling challenged, having responsibility and autonomy with work. The second theory we will examine was posited by Hackman and Oldham and was called Job Characteristics Theory (JCT). JCT claims to have five core job dimensions and three critical psychological states that when taken together have distinct personal work outcomes. As we look at these theories through the lens of two postal employees, keep in mind that often employers will blame employees for poor work performance when actually it's poor job design. As you will see, rather than waiting for their employer to make their job more interesting, our two employees were resourceful and took job design on for themselves.

Theory Background

Herzberg's Two-Factor Theory

Published in 1959, Herzberg's two-factor theory consists of two factors, motivation and hygiene (Abuiyada & Chou, 2012). The motivation factors are intrinsic and generate job satisfaction (Abuiyada & Chou, 2012). The hygiene factors are extrinsic and generate job dissatisfaction (Abuiyada & Chou, 2012). The motivation factors relate to content of the job and the hygiene factors relate to the context of the job (Herzberg, 1974). It is important to note, Herzberg specifies that satisfaction and dissatisfaction are not simply opposites of each other. They are two independent and continuous sequences (Abuiyada & Chou, 2012). The absence of satisfaction does not result in dissatisfaction. It is the absence of no satisfaction that results in satisfaction and the absence of no dissatisfaction that results in dissatisfaction. Therefore, the motivation factors do not influence job dissatisfaction and the hygiene factors do not influence job satisfaction (Abuiyada & Chou, 2012).

URL: https://wikispaces.psu.edu/display/PSYCH484/Fall+2012+Job+design+case, visited on March 28, 2013

JOHNSON ASSOCIATES, INC.
Compensation Consultants

Home | Consulting Services | Recent Press | Select Mailings | Contact Us

Johnson Associates is a boutique compensation consulting firm specializing in the design of annual and long-term incentive plans along with establishing appropriate market levels across a number of industry sectors. Our Firm has a long-standing reputation for providing independent advice to clients with a strong focus on candor and sound judgments.

Our deep industry knowledge and understanding of current market practices and perspectives enables us to provide tailored solutions based on specific business situations, needs and culture.

NEW REPORTS:

URL: http://www.johnsonassociates.com/, visited on March 28, 2013

Xinnovations
better by networking

Start | Medieninformationen | Medienpartner

Programm
W3C Events
Xpitch
Tickets

Sprecher
Momente '12
Sponsoren
Partner

Timeline
Medienservices

Xinnovations 2012: Das Internet als Chancenraum begreifen und besser nutzen

Berlin, 14.09.2012 - Mit einem optimistischen Aufruf zur Gestaltung der Zukunft ist in Berlin das Forum für Internet, Politik und Innovation zu Ende gegangen. An drei Tagen trafen sich in der Humboldt-Universität zu Berlin hochkarätige Expertinnen und Experten aus Wissenschaft, Wirtschaft und Politik, um über Herausforderungen und Gestaltungsmöglichkeiten der Informationsgesellschaft zu diskutieren. Zentrale Themen waren semantische Technologien und ihre Bedeutung für das Internet der Zukunft, die Öffnung von Staat und Gesellschaft im Zeitalter sozialer Medien und Globalisierung sowie die Schaffung eines Klimas für Open Innovation.

Die Veranstalter der Xinnovations freuen sich sehr über den starken Zuspruch der TeilnehmerInnen zum neuen Format. Erstmals wurden in den Foren auch die soziologischen, juristischen und politischen Aspekte der internetbasierten Informationstechnologien gleichrangig thematisiert. Ob des Erfolgs soll der interdisziplinäre Ansatz auch die zukünftigen Programme der Xinnovations prägen."Schließlich darf unzweifelhaft angenommen werden", so der Vorsitzende

CHECKpoint eLearning

innovations monitor
berlin | brandenburg

URL: http://www.xinnovations.de/medienservices.html, visited on March 28, 2013

V. PRESENTATION TO COLLOQUIUM

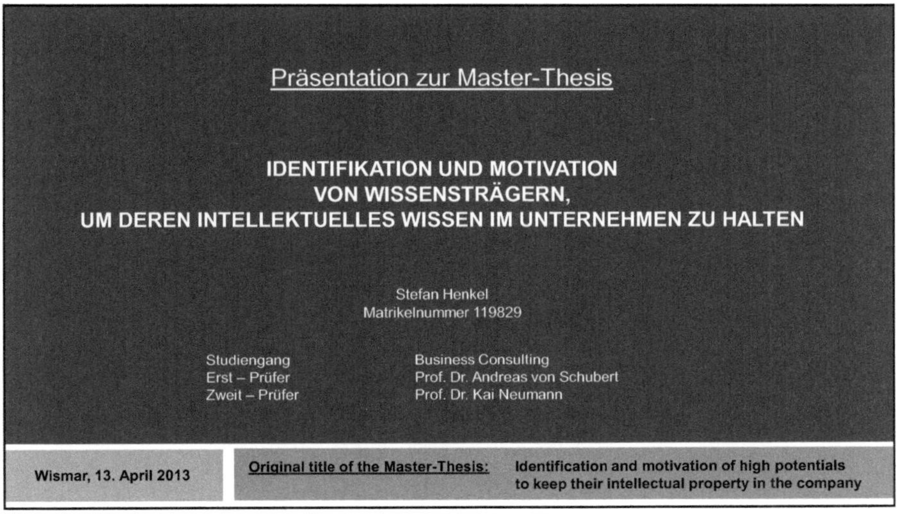

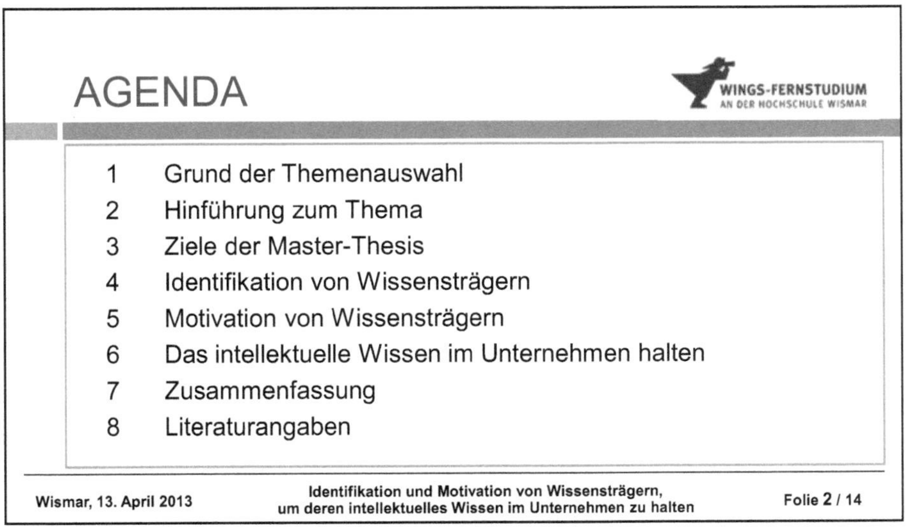

1 Grund der Themenauswahl

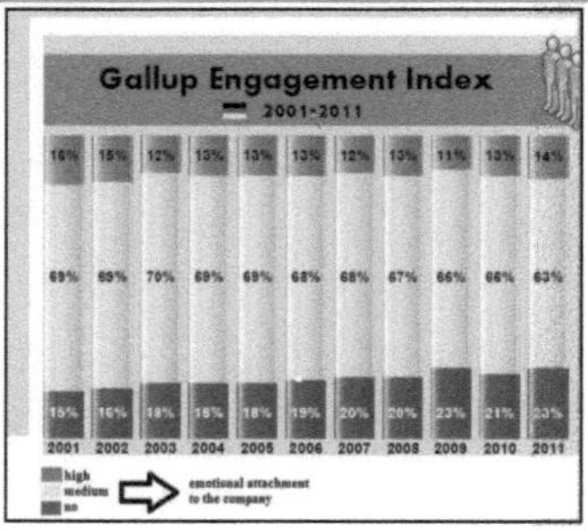

- Zu wenig High Potentials
- Erschreckend hohe Zahl an Mitläufern
- Konstant steigende Zahl an inneren Kündigungen

Quelle: Eigene Darstellung, in Anlehnung an Gallup: Jeder vierte Arbeitnehmer hat innerlich gekündigt, 2011

Wismar, 13. April 2013 | Identifikation und Motivation von Wissensträgern, um deren intellektuelles Wissen im Unternehmen zu halten | Folie 3 / 14

2 Hinführung zum Thema

- **Identifikation** von High Potentials
  - Abgrenzung zu allgemeinen Recruitment-Themen
  - Zielgruppe sind bereits angestellte Mitarbeiter
- **Motivation** von High Potentials
  - Abgrenzung zu Auswahl passender Motivations-Tools
  - Abgrenzung zur Darstellung von Motivationseffekten
  - Beschreibung wie Motivation funktioniert
- Das **intellektuelle Wissen der Mitarbeiter im Unternehmen halten**
  - Abgrenzung zu Kündigungen von Mitläufern und Mitarbeitern, die kein Interesse an der Firma haben
  - Abgrenzung zu Negativeffekten von Kündigungen der High Potentials
  - Darstellung und Auswirkung von den Top 10 Mitarbeiterbindungs-Tools

Wismar, 13. April 2013 | Identifikation und Motivation von Wissensträgern, um deren intellektuelles Wissen im Unternehmen zu halten | Folie 4 / 14

3 Ziele der Master-Thesis

- „Hire and Fire“ ist keine erfolgreiche Personalstrategie
- Identifizierungs-Tool für High Potentials, Mitläufer und innerlich bereits gekündigte Mitarbeiter
- Gruppe der High Potentials vergrößern
- High Potentials in der eigenen Firma halten
- Verstehen wie Motivation funktioniert
- Case Studies sollen als Leitfaden für Human Resources Manager dienen

Wismar, 13. April 2013 | Identifikation und Motivation von Wissensträgern, um deren intellektuelles Wissen im Unternehmen zu halten | Folie 5 / 14

4 Identifikation von Wissensträgern

- ABC-Analyse:
  Einteilung der Mitarbeiter in drei Gruppen
  - Vertretbarkeit des Analyse-Tools
  - Unterscheidung zwischen Nicht-Können und Nicht-Wollen
  - Kriterien: Hard und Soft Skills

→ A-Mitarbeiter bilden den Kern eines Unternehmens und sind hier als gelbe Schnittmenge dargestellt

Wismar, 13. April 2013 | Identifikation und Motivation von Wissensträgern, um deren intellektuelles Wissen im Unternehmen zu halten | Folie 6 / 14

4 Identifikation von Wissensträgern

Die wichtigsten Tools zur Identifizierung von High Potentials

- Beurteilungsgespräche
  - Wozu dient ein Beurteilungsgespräch?
  - Darstellung des Prozesses und der einzelnen Etappen
  - Diverse Formen der Beurteilung

    → Selbsteinschätzung, Bewertung durch Vorgesetzten, 360° Feedback
- Management By Objectives
  - Gemeinesame Vereinbarung von Zielen: S.M.A.R.T.
  - Ziele: Standards und Leistung, Entwicklung, Methoden, Verhalten, Führungsverantwortung

Wismar, 13. April 2013 | **Identifikation und Motivation von Wissensträgern, um deren intellektuelles Wissen im Unternehmen zu halten** | **Folie 7 / 14**

5 Motivation von Wissensträgern

Dieses Kapitel wird in der Master-Thesis mit einer Fallstudie abgeschlossen.

- Funktionsweise von Motivation
  - Unterschied zwischen intrinsischer und extrinsischer Motivation
  - Theorien nach Maslow, Herzberg und McClelland
- Wichtigkeit der Unternehmensmarke
  - Positives Firmenimage steigert die Mitarbeitermotivation
  - Nebeneffekte: Ranking steigt, Recruitierungskosten sinken
- Überlastung und Burnout
  - Starke Zunahme an Fehltagen durch Überlastung und Burnout
  - Deutsche DAX-Firmen geben Auskunft über Krankheitsfälle

Wismar, 13. April 2013 | **Identifikation und Motivation von Wissensträgern, um deren intellektuelles Wissen im Unternehmen zu halten** | **Folie 8 / 14**

5 Motivation von Wissensträgern

Dieses Kapitel wird in der Master-Thesis mit einer Fallstudie abgeschlossen.

- Führungskräfte als Energie-Manager
  - Fordern und Entlasten zur gleichen Zeit
  - Mitarbeiter möchten geködert und gereizt werden
  - Wünsche und Anregungen der Mitarbeiter ernst nehmen
  - Ziele der Führungskräfte und Mitarbeiter sollten überwiegend dacore sein
- Gesetz der Gelassenheit
  - *Gott gebe mir die Gelassenheit, Dinge hinzunehmen, die ich nicht ändern kann,*
    den Mut, Dinge zu ändern, die ich ändern kann,
    und die Weisheit, das eine vom anderen zu unterscheiden.[1]
  - Mitarbeiter sollten in Ihre Stärken, Intelligenz, Know How, Beziehungen und Privates investieren

[1] Quelle: R. Niebuhr, Influential American theologian, philosopher and political scientist, 1941

Wismar, 13. April 2013 | Identifikation und Motivation von Wissensträgern, um deren intellektuelles Wissen im Unternehmen zu halten | Folie 9 / 14

6 Das intellektuelle Wissen im Unternehmen halten

Dieses Kapitel wird in der Master-Thesis mit einer Fallstudie abgeschlossen.

- Wissen schützen durch Mitarbeiterbindung
  - Mitarbeitern mehr bieten als die Konkurrenz
  - Motivationsfaktoren halten High Potentials im Unternehmen
    Gehalt, Umfeld, Perspektiven, Arbeitsatmosphäre, Führungsstil, etc.
- TOP 10 der Mitarbeiterbindungs-Tools[2]
  Berücksichtigt werden die Mitarbeiterstruktur und -bedürfnisse, Unternehmensziele, sowie die Stärken und vorhandenen Ressourcen eines Unternehmens
- Fallstudie zeigt auf wie wichtig es ist, High Potentials im eigenen Unternehmen zu halten und stellt hierfür die entsprechenden Vorgehensweisen dar.

[2] Quelle: C. Liebhart, Mitarbeiterbindung, Employee retention management und die Handlungsfehler der Mitarbeiterbindung, 2009, S. 45

Wismar, 13. April 2013 | Identifikation und Motivation von Wissensträgern, um deren intellektuelles Wissen im Unternehmen zu halten | Folie 10 / 14

6 Das intellektuelle Wissen im Unternehmen halten

Dieses Kapitel wird in der Master-Thesis mit einer Fallstudie abgeschlossen.

TOP 10 der Mitarbeiterbindungs-Tools

1. Aufstiegs- und Entwicklungsmöglichkeiten
2. Professionelle Trainings
3. Verantwortung an High Potentials übertragen
4. Anerkennung und Wertschätzung der Arbeitsleistung
5. Möglichkeiten zur Mitbestimmung und Anteilnahme bei Entscheidungen
6. Leistungsorientierte Vergütung
7. Work Life Balance
8. Perfekte Arbeitsatmosphäre und -umfeld
9. Interne Kommunikation
10. Ehrlichkeit und Glaubwürdigkeit des Unternehmens

Wismar, 13. April 2013 | Identifikation und Motivation von Wissensträgern, um deren intellektuelles Wissen im Unternehmen zu halten | Folie 11 / 14

7 Zusammenfassung

- Eine der schwierigsten strategischen Management-Aufgaben
  - Identifizieren von High Potentials
  - Motivation von High Potentials
  - Intellektuelles Wissen im eigenen Unternehmen halten
- Kündigungen von Mitarbeitern deuten
  - Verlust von Wissen und Potential
  - Stärkung eines Konkurrenten
- In dieser Master-Thesis werden zwei weitere Fragen erarbeitet, die in weiteren wissenschaftlichen Texten bearbeitet werden müssen

  → Aus welchem Grund gibt es noch Unternehmen ohne Motivations-Tools?

  → Aus welchem Grund gibt es nicht nur High Potentials in Unternehmen?

Wismar, 13. April 2013 | Identifikation und Motivation von Wissensträgern, um deren intellektuelles Wissen im Unternehmen zu halten | Folie 12 / 14

8 Literaturangaben der Präsentation

- Gallup Studie, Jeder vierte Arbeitnehmer hat innerlich gekündigt, 2011 http://www.gallup.com/strategicconsulting/158162/gallup-engagement-index.aspx, abgerufen am 11. April 2013
- R. Niebuhr, Influential American theologian, philosopher and political scientist, 1941, erschienen in B. Fening, Kleine Anleitung für mehr Gelassenheit, Schlütersche Verlag, S. 26
- C. Liebhart, Mitarbeiterbindung, Employee retention management und die Handlungsfehler der Mitarbeiterbindung, Druck Diplomica Verlag, Hamburg, 2009, S. 45

Wismar, 13. April 2013 | **Identifikation und Motivation von Wissensträgern, um deren intellektuelles Wissen im Unternehmen zu halten** | **Folie 13 / 14**

Vielen Dank für Ihre Aufmerksamkeit

**IDENTIFIKATION UND MOTIVATION
VON WISSENSTRÄGERN,
UM DEREN INTELLEKTUELLES WISSEN IM UNTERNEHMEN ZU HALTEN**

Stefan Henkel
Matrikelnummer 119829

Wismar, 13. April 2013

Original title of the Master-Thesis: **Identification and motivation of high potentials to keep their intellectual property in the company**